Own Your Business, *Own Your Life!*

21 Strategies for Becoming a Wealthy Entrepreneur™

Phillip K. Wilkins

Boston, Massachusetts
www.AcanthusPublishing.com

Published by Acanthus Publishing
a division of the Ictus Group, LLC
343 Commercial Street
Unit 214, Union Wharf
Boston, MA 02109

Publisher's Cataloging-In-Publication Data
(Prepared by The Donohue Group, Inc.)

Wilkins, Phillip K.
    Own your business, own your life! : 21 strategies for becoming a
    wealthy entrepreneur / Phillip K. Wilkins.

    p. : ill., charts ; cm.

    Includes bibliographical references and glossary.
    ISBN: 1-933631-45-7

    1. Entrepreneurship. 2. Small business--Management. 3. Success in
    business. 4. New business enterprises. 5. Franchises (Retail trade) I.
    Title.

    HD62.5 .W55 2006
    658.4/21

Printed in the United States of America
10 9 8 7 6 5 4 3 2 1

PRAISE FOR
OWN YOUR BUSINESS, *OWN YOUR LIFE!*

"One of the most brilliantly written books in this postmodern era. Phil Wilkins has constructed a detailed roadmap to living a life of significance. I invite you to leverage every tool that he shares with you as you rebuild your world from the inside out."

— Simon T. Bailey, Catalyst of Brilliance, *Imagination Institute, Inc.*

"I have spent a good deal of my life working for groups, like the National Association of Minority Automobile Dealers, that help minority entrepreneurs achieve excellence in their field. Consequently, I am always on the lookout for new authors that I believe will become influential and motivational voices in minority communities. Phil Wilkins is that author. This book is the best I've seen as a how-to guide for anyone to become his or her own boss, regardless of his race, ethnicity, or economic and social status. I would encourage every society, club, or social group to put it on their reading list and then give a copy to their friends."

— Donald P. Tinsley Sr., President of *Legacy Ford, Inc.*, former Chairman and current Treasurer of *National Association of Minority Automobile Dealers*, recipient of *Jesse Jones Vision Award*

"**Own Your Business, *Own Your Life!*** is a true reflection of the steps one needs to take to become a successful entrepreneur. It's about aligning yourself with the correct network of influences, becoming financially stable, and having the passion to succeed."

— Dr. Melvin J. Gravely, Director of the *Institute for Entrepreneurial Thinking*

"This is the best book I've read on how to-do-it strategies for people who are aspiring entrepreneurs. Besides being motivational and inspiring, these 21 Strategies are extremely accessible and interesting. Although Mr. Wilkins concentrates on building a business within a franchise, his advice on managing money and 'owning yourself' is something everyone can benefit from. Whether you are already an entrepreneur, just beginning to look for self-employment opportunities, or simply want to increase your net worth, this book is a must-read for anyone who wants to get out there and make it on his or her own."

— Pat Lottier, Publisher of the *Atlanta Tribune: The Magazine*

"As Chairman and CEO of the largest African American business association in the United States, I highly recommend this incredible book as a must-read for those poised and ready for survival in the twenty-first

century. We as a people will never fully succeed financially in America while working for someone other than ourselves."
— Ernie Adair, Chairman and CEO of *National Black McDonald's® Operators Association*

"Those of us who look for more than do-it-yourself platitudes in a business book finally have a guide to entrepreneurship that truly captures everything today's aspiring small business owner needs to know. Phil understands that it takes more than just 'entrepreneurial spirit' to successfully make the move from corporate America. His 21 Strategies demonstrate how to translate the entrepreneurial must-haves – courage and discipline – into a sound business plan that will put you in the driver's seat on the road to career and life success."
— Bob Kustka, President of *CHR Partners*, founder of the *Fusion Factor™*, former HR Executive of *The Gillette Company*

"The 21 Strategies this book lays out are incredibly practical and helpful, even for old dogs like me. It is a great resource and I would recommend it to anyone interested in starting his or her own business or anyone just looking for economic empowerment... I loved it!"
— Adam Troy, CEO of *Troy Enterprises* and President of *Omni Management Group*

"Phil's book is deeply inspirational – a clarion call to those of us who want more from our work than just a paycheck. Whether you have always dreamed of being your own boss or you are wondering how to escape the corporate grind, this book can give you a head-start on your future *and* keep you from making costly mistakes. In these pages, you will find easy-to-implement strategies that will help you build the business – and the life – you want."
— Eve B. Rose, President of *Rose Communications, Inc.*

"This book tells the timeless story of sacrifice, hard work, discipline, and delayed rewards but with a renewed authenticity rooted in the honest confession of one who learned that lesson for himself. Phil compels the reader to listen and then Phil challenges the reader to replicate his achievements. But what I love most about Phil and his book is that he never loses sight of the most important things in life. An invaluable resource for the business and financial tips alone, **Own Your Business, Own Your Life!** becomes an inspirational must-read with its message that success is not a solitary journey."
— Wil Spencer, President and CEO of *New England Minority Supplier Development Council*

ACKNOWLEDGEMENTS

I am very thankful to have a great support base. I would first like to thank God for the opportunity and blessings that have been abundant in my life. I also thank my wife for all of her unwavering love, support, and encouragement, my sons for making the job of fatherhood so much fun (you three are the reason I do what I do), and finally my dad and sister for their love and support.

I also want to thank my business manager, Teresa, and my director of operations, Ron. The flexibility and freedom I enjoy would not be possible if it were not for these two special individuals. Teresa and Ron are my rocks, and I have truly been blessed to have such great people on my team.

Special thanks to Nathan Mack, whose friendship and understanding of finances is truly a gift and has been a blessing to me, and to Susan Sadr, my financial advisor, who has helped mentor and coach me in my consulting practice as well as my financial affairs. Brian Scott and Jeff Copeland, your friendship and mentoring over the years has been a great blessing. Simon T. Bailey, our weekly calls are something I always look forward to and I am proud of you and your accomplishments. And Denise White, a great friend who always finds ways to get me involved in the community.

And finally, I need to thank the fine folks at Acanthus Publishing: Paige, Tony, Catherine, and Alison, you all have been awesome to work with and you are all great at what you do.

Thank You!

TABLE OF CONTENTS

FOREWORD

In June 2004, I attended the Merrill Lynch African American Financial Advisor Training Symposium and saw Phil Wilkins speak for the first time. Phil, then just beginning his public speaking career, was impressive, and I knew he was a person I wanted to meet. Here was an entrepreneur who could relate to a corporate audience, who could speak about business and life matters in an engaging style, who had personally lived through the experience of saving up for his dreams, and who had built a business and significant net wealth from scratch. As Phil finished, I joined the rest of the audience in a standing ovation and approached him later in the conference.

Today, as Phil's friend and occasional mentor, I am pleased to introduce his first book, one that I believe should be required reading for anyone interested in starting a business, gaining control of his or her life, or simply looking for tips to increase net worth.

Combining humorous anecdotes with inspirational lessons from behind the counter, Phil takes the reader through his journey of starting a business from the ground up to ultimately running one of the most successful McDonald's® franchises in the nation. Along the way, he lays out 21 tried and tested strategies that allow anyone, regardless of previous business experience, to begin a career as an entrepreneur and start making more money. But what makes this book so compelling is the fact that Phil literally started from the bottom and, through hard work and sacrifice, made his way to the top.

Phil left corporate America to follow his dream of owning his own business. Armed with financial knowledge but little entrepreneurial experience, Phil had to learn how to be the boss through trial and error, with a little help from his mentors along the way. Consequently, the tips Phil gives in **Own Your Business**, *Own Your Life* are truly invaluable – he's personally used them to achieve his own success. Phil's book covers all the bases. From how to read and understand income statements, to how to hire the best team possible, to how to create diverse wealth systems, this well-rounded book is sure to offer everyone, regardless of their current financial understanding, new knowledge that will enhance their business savvy.

Phil's lead-off strategy, "Choose to Be a Wealthy Entrepreneur," sets readers on a solid path toward business ownership. It also dispenses valuable advice about owning one's own *life* through entrepreneurship. Phil calls on his readers to examine their current financial picture and shows them that they have the ability to control their financial destiny.

Who wouldn't want to be his own boss, increase net worth, set her own hours, and gain financial freedom? Read this book and get ready to *own your business and your life*!

> – Kelvin Boston, host of PBS's *Moneywise with Kelvin Boston* and author of *Smart Money Moves for African Americans*

INTRODUCTION

The purpose of **Own Your Business,** *Own Your Life!* is to provide you with strategies to assist in your development as a business owner. I am amazed by how many small, mundane details I am required to know as a business owner, how my corporate job did very little to prepare me for running my own business, and the impact business ownership can have on your life and relationships.

This book will provoke thought and dialogue between you, your spouse, and other members of your team. Now is the time to answer the tough questions and to determine whether or not you have the passion and the aptitude to be a Wealthy Entrepreneur.

Becoming an entrepreneur has been a great experience for me. I am motivated and passionate about my business and I enjoy the flexibility and freedom that comes with being the "boss."

I would like to help other people achieve these privileges. But this flexibility and freedom can, and has, ruined businesses where the solid foundation of discipline was not established. By sharing common sense approaches to running a small business, I believe I can assist people in successfully creating wealth for themselves and their loved ones through entrepreneurship.

Entrepreneurship is not for everyone and corporate America can be, and is, a great opportunity for many people. If you stay on the corporate side, I would encourage you to begin to build an asset base outside of your employment. This may be something small, such as a network marketing business or rental real estate, but you should have something that you are slowly building outside of your current job in order to create an independent source of financial security. As a result of running your own business, you will not only become a better employee, but you will have options in case things don't work out at your company.

I hope you enjoy and use this book well into the future to reach your goal of becoming a Wealthy Entrepreneur.

−Phil

My Story

I wrote this book for the corporate professional and the person who is aspiring to own a business and take control of his or her life. I used to be a corporate professional, and those are the people I know. I also know many people who would enjoy running their own businesses, but because of the failure rate and/or the "golden handcuffs," they don't want to take the risk. That's certainly understandable.

I tell my friends who are in high-profile jobs to stick with it. If your ticket is being punched, the money is good, and your career is on track, ride that pony as long as you can. Heck, if my career had stayed on track, I may not have taken the entrepreneurial route. Now that I've taken it, however, I find that I love it and wouldn't want to return. But you don't know what you're missing unless you experience it.

Many of the brightest people in this country work for corporations and run someone else's business with great efficiency and effectiveness. Although these employees keep the business running, it's the business owner who reaps most of the profits and who often enjoys greater job flexibility and freedom.

That was hard as hell for me to believe as a new entrepreneur! When I first started my business, I took a sixty-seven percent pay cut, and worked on average twelve hours per day, seven days a week. I actually felt I was *losing* ground to my peers, until my accountant asked me to calculate how much money I would have to make to acquire enough stock in the company I used to work for to equal the equity I was accumulating in my own business.

When I calculated the numbers and realized the figure would have been greater than $700,000, I became secure in my decision. Few people make that much money working for someone else, and eventually, after three years, my schedule and income improved.

Starting Down the Corporate Path

My corporate career started at Procter & Gamble, and I must say I am very grateful to that company and the people I worked with. I interned with them in college, and that made my transition to a full-time employee easy after graduation.

As a result of that internship, I was able to see New York City for the first time. Having this real world work experience while still in college enhanced my understanding of my management classes tremendously. Working at Procter & Gamble also exposed me to mutual funds, stocks, bonds, and real estate.

I had never heard of mutual funds before I started that job. But they interested me, and I began to read about investing because my co-workers kept talking about *their* investment portfolios. I remember reading the rule of "seventy-two" (where you divide seventy-two by your interest rate and that equals the number of years it will take for your money to double) and had to pull out my calculator to see if it was true.

I was both exited and discouraged to learn this rule. On average, the stock market returns ten to eleven percent annually, so if I had $1,000 invested and received a ten percent return, it would take more than seven years for my money to double. I began to think about faster ways to generate wealth and I often thought of owning my own business or buying real estate, but I couldn't imagine how I would go about it.

Caught Up in the Trappings

During this time, I also learned the advantages of home ownership versus renting, and the dangers of installment debt. During my eighteen months at Procter & Gamble, I spent a lot of money on the trendy East End apartment I rented. My college car, a Chrysler Cordoba, was no longer good enough

– I had to have a two-seat sports car that was more appropriate for my bachelor lifestyle, and less appropriate for my budget.

I was caught up in having all of the trappings of success. "Fake it till you make it" was my mantra, and I lived it. My money was spent before I went to work. I was an economic slave. Finance charges and poor personal decisions were my bondage, and I was living well beyond my means.

I did, however, grow professionally during those months at Procter & Gamble. I quickly learned that promotions don't just happen; you have to initiate them. I also discovered how important image was for an employee and his or her employer. We were very conservative then: winged-tip shoes; blue, gray, or brown suits; and ultra-starched shirts. In a room full of a thousand people you could tell the "Proctoids." People expressed their individuality by their ties, a piece of jewelry, or an expensive pen. Only my Mont Blanc pen would do and, of course, I eventually left it in my shirt pocket and accidentally threw it in the washing machine. To this day, I have not replaced it.

After eighteen months at Procter & Gamble, I moved to Baxter Healthcare, where I enjoyed a lucrative career in sales. I also learned about restructuring in large corporations, and its impact on job security and mental stability. Unfortunately, I joined the company during the healthcare reform years. Business was turbulent and no job seemed to be safe from the corporate cost-cutting axe.

During one of those years, Baxter implemented

a thirty percent commission cut for straight commissioned representatives. Fortunately, I hadn't reached that status and so avoided the sting of that decision. But it reinforced an important lesson: Live within your means. Those impacted by the commission cut were financially devastated and had to drastically change their lifestyles. Many had to sell boats, second homes, and other "toys" to stay afloat. When I saw this, I knew that many of my peers who were caught up in the trappings of success were in trouble. Fortunately, by this time I had cleaned up my act and was financially responsible.

Living above your means is economic slavery. I remember one guy I used to work with who sold his stock each month to pay his house note. How crazy is that? I would much rather build my net worth by living in a smaller home or by driving a more practical car than live lavishly and grow my net debt.

Fate Calls

During my tenure at Baxter, I often dreamed of owning my own business, but I couldn't imagine leaving the company. Despite the turbulence of the industry, I was making great money and I had fun working for the company. They promoted me from a sales representative in a rural market to an urban market, then to area training manager, then finally to the sales manager of the Cincinnati region. My career was headed in the right direction. I felt safe and confident. Then I received a phone call from my division president.

That phone call, followed by his visit two weeks later, shook any illusions I had about my security as a corporate employee. During his visit, he informed me that my region was merging with the Indianapolis branch, and he didn't feel I had the experience to lead both. Although he let me stay with the company, I had to accept a demotion, moving back into sales and into another division of the company. I wanted to stay in Cincinnati, where there were now no open management positions, so I took what I could get.

During the transition to my new job, I read an article in *Money* magazine that changed my life. It was about an owner of two McDonald's® restaurants in California who had previously lost his job and who also happened to be African American. As I read this story, I knew instantly that this article was meant for me and that this was what I was going to do.

I had been dreaming of owning my own business since graduating from college because my family is full of entrepreneurs. I had uncles who own their own barbershops, one who has a milk hauling business, and another who owns a car dealership. But still, I could never seem to figure out what *I* would want to do. All that changed when I read this article. I had never worked in a restaurant, but McDonald's® was known for its great training. Plus, this was a business I could relate to – food!

I honestly read that article over a hundred times and could recite the key highlights as if they were my own – I even visualized myself as the subject!

As I read it again and again, I started to become passionate about pursuing franchise ownership. I began to network and seek out people who owned McDonald's® franchises, read every book I could get my hands on that dealt with the business, and carried that edition of *Money* magazine around with me for years, taking it on cruises, to bed, and even to meetings.

Because the gentleman featured in the article had lost his job, he was able to complete the training program in one year by pursuing it full time. By the end of his training, he was allowed to lease his first restaurant for $66,000. I was only twenty-five years old at the time, so that seemed like an extraordinary amount of money to me, but also a great deal for a brand as well-known as McDonald's®. My only problem was my total net worth: $20,000, including that broken Mont Blanc pen. Of that meager amount, a large portion was tied up in retirement funds and equity in my home, and I needed $66,000 in *cash*.

Getting Going By Networking

Despite my shortcomings, this story excited and motivated me, and I began to network to learn more about my options. I had a great relationship with my insurance agent, and he knew practically everyone in my hometown. I asked him if he knew anyone who managed or owned a McDonald's® and he put me in touch with a gentleman named Mr. Jones.

I had played football with his son in high school,

so Mr. Jones and I immediately hit it off. He introduced me to an owner of six McDonald's® in Hamilton, Ohio, who introduced me to the licensing manager for the region.

Through this networking, I was able to meet decision makers within the business. Here I was with no money, yet talking with influential names in the company and I hadn't even applied for a franchise yet – I was just exploring! But the more I met with the representatives, the more I knew this was what I wanted to do.

Networking is a skill that I have learned over the years. Many people are not comfortable "playing the game," but it is the way business is done. I can honestly say that networking occupies a large portion of my time. I am convinced that everyone has a million dollars or more in his or her Rolodex. It's just a matter of finding the right person at the right time with the right deal.

Networking for Wealthy Entrepreneurs is so important because people do business with people they like – those with whom they can relate and know will get the job done. Managers also promote people they are comfortable with. Therefore, figure out your strengths. Use them to make yourself more enticing to the people you meet or to make your manager notice you.

Throughout this process of networking, I was amazed at how people were willing to help me. I learned a valuable lesson that I will take with me for the rest of my life: People are willing to help those who are willing to help themselves. If you approach people with a desire to learn and improve, people – regardless of age, sex, race, or religion – will bend over backwards to help you. This has happened to me on countless occasions, and every time it happens I am humbled by all the goodness that is in this world.

Finally, after this extensive networking, my wife and I applied for a franchise and had two or three formal interviews. Once they reviewed our finances, however, we were rejected. When I received the letter of rejection, I was disappointed because I felt like a failure. I had lost my sales management position, the job I coveted, and now I couldn't even buy a job!

Not Giving Up Without a Fight

As I sat at the kitchen table sulking, something within me said to call the licensing manager. I had spent the past four years in sales and I knew that when a *customer* rejected you, you closed the gap to find the real reason for the rejection. Plus, owning my own business was my dream and I was not going to give it up easily.

I called the licensing manager and surprisingly got him on the first try. He was very calm in explaining to me that my wife and I were good candidates, but unfortunately so were others with greater financial resources. He asked if I could get a gift from my parents. I told him my father worked five jobs to provide for us, and that this was my dream, not his.

Shortly after that statement, he indicated that

there was nothing else he could do, so I asked him the "gap question." Is the lack of financial resources the only reason for our rejection? "Yes" was all he said. That was great. I knew that, given time, my finances were something I could change. So, I asked him if he'd mind if I stayed in contact with him despite the rejection. He had no problem with that, so I thanked him and I hung up the phone.

I am so thankful I called him. How many people take the easy road and give up their dreams after their first rejection or significant hurdle? But it's perseverance that makes great entrepreneurs. Where would Oprah Winfrey, Henry Ford, Ray Kroc, Walt Disney, Colonel Sanders, or Bob Johnson be if they gave up after hitting their first obstacle? If you are committed and believe in your goal, you have to keep going despite the rejections or oppositions you face.

Once I realized that, despite this rejection, my dream was still alive, I became possessed. I was a man on a mission! I was a pit bull chasing after someone who stole his food. I was willing to do whatever it took to the raise the money and realize my dream. My wife and I paid off all of our installment debt, cut our expenses, and buckled down on our careers. We were always serious about our professions, but we saw this as an opportunity and we worked together to make it happen.

I began writing the licensing manager every other month and detailing our financial progress. It was truly gratifying to watch our finances improve and see how accurate I was at projecting our future saving targets. I rarely missed a goal, and these weren't conservative targets. I had discovered a routine and a system for investing, and it was working.

I invested our money in my stock plan, earning fifteen percent, and any excess cash went into a tax-exempt money market fund. I also continued to invest in our retirement plans, where I could contribute up to twelve percent of my earnings and my wife could contribute up to sixteen percent of her wages.

Our friends used to tease us about our old cars and our floor model televisions. We had no big screen TV and our little house had avocado-green kitchen fixtures. However, we were determined to reach our financial goal, so we consciously delayed any material gratification. While everyone we knew was in the upgrade stage of his or her life and career, my wife and I were downgrading, trying to save money to buy our own business.

Fork in the Road

As my wife and I scraped and slaved to save money, life threw me another difficult decision. Another company offered me a job that would increase my base salary by thirty-four percent, provide me with twenty-five percent of my salary in up-front stock, and allow me to relocate. The golden handcuffs were swinging before my eyes, and believe me, I was tempted.

I wanted to get back into management, but I also

wanted to own my own business. Relocating and getting back on the fast track would further delay my dream or perhaps eliminate it altogether. I was flattered by the opportunity, but we had also saved enough money by that point to begin the training program. McDonald's® hadn't called, though. I agonized over my decision for a month and the more I talked about the opportunity, the more attractive it became. I drove my wife crazy tossing and turning trying to make up my mind.

Finally, I called McDonald's® and asked if I was even close to being accepted into the training program. In typical corporate style, they were noncommittal, only saying that the job offer appeared to be an excellent opportunity and I should do what was best for my family. But if I relocated to another part of the country, there was no guarantee that a McDonald's® in that region would be willing to accept me.

After our conversation, I considered the job offer for a few more days, then called the recruiter and declined. He thought I was crazy and he wasn't alone. I thought I was crazy too! But I was committed to owning my own business and determined to see it through.

Relying on Faith

It had been three years since our initial rejection by McDonald's®. I talk about having faith as an entrepreneur, and I guess my faith and belief in myself and in this business became evident to a lot of people when I rejected that job offer. It was tough, because I knew I had a few more years of working in a job that underutilized me. I had been in sales before, and I was ready for a new challenge. As another three or four months passed without a word from McDonald's®, however, I worried that I had made the wrong choice.

Therefore, you can imagine how thrilled I was when McDonald's® finally called to accept me into the ownership training program! By then, our net worth had improved five times over and our free cash had also improved enough to be able to lease the restaurant at that point, if needed.

Being accepted into the training program or becoming a registered applicant doesn't guarantee you a franchise. It just allows you to work in the restaurant and learn their system of running a business. That was exciting because it was a chance for me to prove myself, but very tough because I also had to maintain my full-time job at Baxter while learning this business.

With a four-state sales territory, I was on the road a minimum of two or three nights a week. Fridays were exceptionally demanding, because I literally changed from my suit and tie to my McDonald's® gear and worked there until close. Then I woke up on Saturdays and Sundays and did it again. This went on for three years, without one dime of compensation.

Yes, I worked at McDonald's® for three years without pay! I cooked burgers, made fries, cleaned toilets, handled customer complaints, learned how to schedule employees, and worked with owners. I was exposed to every facet of the business and knew it well when they finally awarded me my own restaurant.

During this time, my employer continued to restructure the organization in response to the uneasy business climate in the healthcare industry. I knew no sales job was safe in this industry, but now I didn't worry because I was following my own personal plan. Yes, if my job had been cut during this time it would have hurt. But because my wife and I were now living below our means, losing one of our incomes wouldn't have been devastating.

Meanwhile, as my McDonald's® training progressed, I was amazed to find that I became a better Baxter employee. I had a greater understanding of business, and as a result, ran my sales territory more like a business. Baxter rewarded me with an incredible incentive trip to Maui and I was able to surpass my financial goals, making more money than ever.

Consequently, I think companies should encourage employees to have their own small business, because I was shocked at how much goes into making a business run smoothly. (Think of something as basic as electricity. You come into your office on Monday morning, hit the switch, and the lights come on. Who pays for that? I never had to think about electricity costs as a corporate employee, but as a small business owner, I do. If more individuals owned their own business, you can best be sure that they would consider these daily small expenses.) Often as an employee, all you see is that you are only being compensated a small percentage of your region, division, or company's revenue, because you don't understand all of the other costs associated with running a business. As I became more fiscally educated, I still didn't appreciate the minimal amount of my compensation, but at least I began to recognize all the other expenses required to run a business.

Many companies, public or private, only expose their employees to certain line items of the income statement, if they show anything at all. As a result, companies have individuals who run divisions but still don't understand business basics. I share with my store managers everything they control (sales, cost of goods, gross profit, utilities, maintenance, repairs, etc.) and my business manager and director of operations see the entire profit and loss statement.

One of the aspects of the McDonald's® training that I valued most was the opportunity to work with a variety of owners and establish mentoring relationships. How valuable would it be in corporate America for everyone to have a mentor in the organization who would be willing to share the highs and lows of his or her career and coach you with your best interests at heart?

When I met with other McDonald's® owners and worked in their restaurants, we had an opportunity to talk one-on-one. I cherished that opportunity. I knew that when they told me about their experiences, they were giving it to me straight.

Their stories weren't always comforting, but at least I knew what to expect when I opened my own franchise. Entrepreneurs need mentors and advisors just as employees do. I often relied on the expertise and advice of my mentors during my first few years as an owner. It was comforting to talk with people who had gone through and survived the struggles I now faced.

One of the keys to my success has always been having mentors, or at least an informal advisory board, to help me gain success in an industry or provide me with knowledge and insight into an area of interest. Mentors and coaches still play a vital role in my personal and professional development and, when appropriate, I would recommend finding mentors who can help you advance your business and career.

Full Speed Ahead

In December of 1996, I negotiated a severance package from Baxter and spent the next six months working in a restaurant full-time to understand the volume patterns of the business and the systems.

Working full-time in a restaurant (even though they still weren't paying me) was the best thing I could have done. When people hear that, they think I'm crazy. I say, if you're willing to do something for free, you have a passion! Follow your passion and the material wealth will follow.

Likewise, I knew when I started my consulting practice that I would also be in this area for the long haul because it is another passion. When I first started the business, I did quite a few engagements for free. The gratis work taught me what type of engagements I enjoyed and what industries and people were receptive to my message.

I enjoy the rush I get speaking to a group of sales professionals or business owners and making a difference in their lives. I also enjoy the thrill of getting paid! For me, there is nothing like the excitement of a firm or a client paying me for my expertise and for doing something that I genuinely enjoy. And every time I have an engagement, I am grateful and thankful, and my wife and I celebrate in some small way. When you add value, you should be paid! I'm a firm believer that if you find your passion, you will make more money and enjoy more career and life success because you will be doing what you love.

The operator who trained me at McDonald's® those final six months has had a tremendous impact on my organization. I actually modeled my business after his. He has ingrained his passion for customer service into my mind, and now I firmly believe that in business, the focus should be on the customer. If I call one of my restaurants and they're busy, I want them to hang up and call me back after the rush. They need to focus on the customer. In our organization, I have a central office that handles the orientation of each new employee and we manage all of the paperwork there to reduce the administrative burden on the managers and their staffs. I can't stress it enough: Focus on the customer!

To me, the greatest compliment any business can receive from a customer is to be called consistently good. Being consistent means your managers and people are trained and your systems are working. It usually also means that you are customer driven and running a profitable business.

Entrepreneurs At Last

After a total of six years of waiting and training, my wife and I purchased our first restaurant in Cincinnati in July 1997. Our discipline had paid off! Our savings had exploded; our free and unencumbered cash of $10,000 jumped to over $250,000 in six years! We also didn't have to lease our first restaurant after all, which meant we could begin gaining equity right away. You can accomplish anything with a plan and a strong faith! We went conventional and put twenty-five percent into the deal. I was nervous, excited, and exhausted. When we wired the money to McDonald's®, I became physically ill, and had to lie down for a couple of hours to regain my composure.

I was so focused on accumulating the resources to buy the business that when it came time to hand the money over, I almost didn't want to do it! Once I became an operator, it took a long time to figure out what to do next.

You see, I was so focused on becoming an entrepreneur that I had lost focus on the real reason for being in business, which is to make money. My first three years as an owner were less than stellar because of this attitude. I was just happy to reach my goal.

Then a better McDonald's® franchise opportunity opened up in Lexington, Kentucky. I was able to trade my store in Cincinnati for one in Lexington and moved, excited to now own two stores. However, once we arrived, I began to see how far in the hole I was. It was scary. I had accepted mediocre performance in Cincinnati, and now it was costing me $150,000 to clean up the mess. Moving was the best thing that ever could have happened to me. I learned that when you close a business, bills continue to come, and if you've had financial shortcomings, they will follow you into your next venture or retirement.

I arrived in Lexington planning to buy an additional restaurant, one that desperately needed to be rebuilt. So, in addition to opening a restaurant, training staff, and moving to a new city, I also had to deal with contractors to build a brand new restaurant from scratch. In the interim, I combined the staff from the now torn-down restaurant into my existing restaurant. I wanted both management teams with me so that I could assess talent, explain my expectations, and ultimately have two restaurants running at peak efficiency.

However, this was incredibly challenging. Initially, the staffs from the two businesses were competing against one another and I really had to lay down the law. I had invested heavily in their training and wanted to build their professionalism.

I was tough on my managers. I wanted them to

understand that they must constantly perform and impart to them the desire to always improve. It was hard, but I had to put some long-term managers on probation and release others. But I was not going to make the same mistake twice.

My managers were not comfortable with change and I could understand. Many of them had worked for the previous company for ten years or more, so the change was hard. Many felt like the previous owner no longer wanted them to be part of his team, which wasn't true. He was just making a business decision to scale down his operation, and these stores were the most logical starting point.

I had to explain to them that my business was in its infancy, that I had a lot of debt and had taken great risks. I told them that they were going to be accountable for the profitability and operations of their restaurant. Many felt I was asking too much and being greedy, but I explained to them that I am in business to make money, not to run a charity. (I had learned my lesson.) Today, those same managers who said my expectations were unrealistic have improved their income statements by as much as eight percent annually and are disappointed when they fail to meet their new levels of performance criteria.

Hiring Great Talent

During this time, I learned the importance of making smart hiring decisions. I hired my business manager from Ohio, Teresa, to help with the transition to Kentucky and to help me lay a foundation of structure and systems in my business. We changed the computer system so we could understand the reporting. We changed the procedure for banking, handling customer complaints, and work requests in the restaurants. A lot of work was being done by unqualified relatives and work was not up to code, so all future work orders had to be called into the office and placed by Teresa.

During my years in Cincinnati, it had become apparent that I wasn't very good at managing the volumes of paperwork business ownership required. Teresa proved to be an excellent hire, because she had complementary skills. She enjoyed the day-to-day back office function of running a business. Plus, she had previously worked for a McDonald's® owner and came highly recommended.

Prior to Teresa's arrival in July 2000, I would work in the restaurant all day and pay bills at night. There was limited time for family and my relationship with my wife was strained. Hiring Teresa was the beginning of owning my life! I could now focus on operations, management development, and most importantly, my family.

As we acquired additional restaurants, I realized that I needed a technical expert, someone who had once been a manager. Although my operational training was solid, I had never "run" a restaurant. I knew what my expectations were, but I didn't exactly know how to get there. Again, I was fortunate to connect with great talent.

Ron was a man I'd always admired. He was a business consultant with McDonald's® Corporation in Lexington, and I saw what a great job he did for them. Ron eventually approached his managers about leaving the corporation and working for an operator, and indicated he would like to work with me. They granted us permission to talk and Ron joined our organization in January of 2001.

Both Teresa and Ron are outstanding at what they do. They take care of the business and are incredible professionals. I am truly blessed to have them on my team and I would stack them up against anyone. They also share the vision of operational excellence and have a great understanding for why we are in business: to make money.

Looking Back

Fortunately, the managers and the local community in Lexington responded well to my ownership, and I'm very thankful for having the opportunity to live and work there. In two years, we grew from one restaurant to four, and today our restaurants are ranked within the top twenty percent of all U.S. McDonald's® restaurants in terms of operations and profitability.

People often ask me how I did it. Many say they wouldn't do what I did and it was dumb for me to work for free. I point out to them that this was an investment in my future for a limited period of time. However, the wealth I could create by becoming a business owner could last for generations.

Sometimes I'm not even sure how we did it. I say "we" because this was a team effort. The training period was equally tough for my wife, because she worked full-time and we had our first child, who demanded a lot of time and energy. He had colic, nine ear infections by the time he was nine months old, and chicken pox at ten months. It was horrible. Especially since I was gone three or four nights a week and at McDonald's® on the weekends.

Needless to say, we were both tired and irritable at times. But we stuck it out and found a way to make it. That is one reason I stress owning your life in addition to owning your business. Owning a business is tough and it impacts the whole family. It's critical that family members be on board with you, because it's very difficult for a household to run smoothly while one spouse is trying to be an entrepreneur.

My mother had a difficult time understanding my rationale and at times her objection was tough to hear. She had lived her whole life with little or no risk and couldn't understand how I was willing to potentially lose everything I'd worked for.

My father, on the other hand, was just the opposite. When I'd mentioned to him what I intended to do, his response was, "Go for it!" He had always wanted to own real estate in my hometown, but my mother discouraged it because she didn't want to be bothered with problems from the renters.

I remember talking to my father one day and complaining about the amount of debt I had to carry to buy the business. He put it all into perspective. He told me that at least I had the opportunity to carry the debt, and it is good debt, which builds wealth. He went on to tell me that when he was younger those opportunities didn't exist for minorities, so I'd better shut up and run with this opportunity!

I never complained again. I never realized how well he grasped what I was doing. Today, we both own property in my hometown and I have been very impressed by his business skills. I know he is proud of me and I am equally proud and grateful for the valuable lessons I have learned from him.

I also now understand that anyone can own his or her own business. However, too many people struggle, failing to create wealth, and at the end of the day, the business owns them, not the other way around. That's not fair to you or to your family. So read on, and follow my 21 Strategies to learn not only how to own your own business, but also how to own your life!

STRATEGY 1

CHOOSE TO BE A
WEALTHY ENTREPRENEUR

I have a lot of admiration for my Uncle Don.
Here's a guy who was born in rural Kentucky, didn't
grow up with much, had no formal education, yet
was able to channel his passion, hard work, and
determination into a thriving small business. He
owns a successful automobile dealership outside
Cleveland, and even rose to become Chairman of
the National Association of Minority Automobile
Dealers, an organization that helps minority auto
dealers succeed and helps automakers attract and
retain minority dealers.

One day when I was visiting Uncle Don's
dealership, he took me out back to a large building
that had been planned as a fitness club, but never
opened. He told me he'd bought the building and
was planning to turn it into a large truck paint and

repair shop. I looked around at the unfinished tennis and racquetball courts and wondered how he'd ever make it work. A year later, he took me on a tour of the building again, and sure enough, he'd turned it into a thriving truck shop.

My Uncle Don is a real inspiration to me. He's a great example of the power of positive dreaming, and how much you can achieve when you execute your passion and turn your dreams into reality.

And Uncle Don isn't alone. According to the Small Business Administration census in 2004, almost *all* U.S. businesses with employees – 99.7 percent of the total 5.7 million businesses – were *small* businesses (companies with fewer than 500 employees). That means small businesses are a major contributor to the U.S. economy; they employ half of all private sector employees and create more than fifty percent of non-farm private gross domestic product (GDP).

It seems that even though thirty-three percent of small businesses fail after the first two years, and less than half survive four or more years, the idea of owning one's own business appeals to *lots* of Americans.

Given the failure rate, why do so many individuals consider going into business for themselves? While there are a variety of reasons, I believe recent events in our history have increased job insecurity for many employees, and made small business ownership an even more attractive option. These include the September 11, 2001 terrorist attacks, high profile cases of corporate malfeasance, and increased demand from Wall Street for continuous improvement in quarterly earnings performance.

Minorities are also entering the small business market faster than ever before. According to the U.S. Census Bureau (www.census.gov), minorities own approximately fifteen percent of all small businesses today. Their data shows that while the national growth rate for business start-ups is ten percent, African American start-ups are growing at a rate of forty-five percent, Hispanic start-ups are growing at a rate of thirty-one percent, and Asian start-ups at twenty-four percent.

Reasons for this phenomenon could include population shifts. However, I'd like to explore five other recent contributing factors that I believe would motivate anyone even toying with the idea of opening a business to give it a try. They include:

- ✓ Corporate Restructuring
- ✓ Stock Market Volatility
- ✓ Corporate Misconduct
- ✓ Interest Rate Volatility
- ✓ Social Security

Corporate Restructuring

Corporate restructuring has, and will continue to have, a dramatic impact on small business development as companies both large and small continually strive to meet expectations for earnings performance. And as employers keep focusing on earnings and stock performance, job reductions and personnel reallocations – actions that are aimed at increasing corporate efficiency – will no doubt continue. As an employee of a large medical supply company, I became accustomed to witnessing restructuring and job cuts every year. I knew that during the holiday season, not all was good cheer. The longer I stayed in my position, the more concerned I became about my own future. We even had a saying in our office, "Keep your options open and your payments low." I never forgot that saying and I still live by it to this day. Even as an entrepreneur where I am responsible for my own destiny, I never let my guard down.

What employees must recognize is that all the stock options, company cars, and unique benefits can vanish quickly if the business unit no longer fits into the company's business equation. It's not personal, it's business. And it's not easy for executives to do. In fact, it is very difficult. As a small business owner, I've had to restructure my own organization and I didn't enjoy doing it. But in the long-term, I felt it was best for the organization and for the people involved to gain a fresh start somewhere else. As an employee, you can never assume you're safe from possible job elimination, and as a business owner, you can't assume you won't face tough times.

Stock Market Volatility
In the 1990s, the stock market and the economy boomed. Many people reached financial levels

they'd never dreamed possible thanks to initial public offerings, stock options, and stock splits. But when the dot-com bubble burst around 2000, the party was over for investors. The 9/11 terrorist attacks in 2001 then sent the stock market reeling. We all learned the hard lesson of "what goes up must come down." We felt vulnerable. This made a lot of people more willing to consider starting small businesses they could control – it certainly pushed me in that direction. Starting my own business seemed like a viable option versus riding out the ups and downs of the market and its impact on my large employer.

Despite the volatility, however, I still encourage people to continue to invest in stocks on a regular basis. Just be sure to choose solid companies with strong earnings and reputations. I recall buying one stock of a consumer products firm after it had missed earnings expectations. The stock price had fallen substantially in a short period of time, but I still felt it was a well-run company with a solid business model, so I invested. The stock has since rebounded significantly and I've enjoyed watching the company improve and my investment grow.

But I'm no stock-picking pro. I invested in another company I knew little about and had conducted limited research on, and I've paid the price as I watched this company's stock price decrease more than sixty dollars per share before I sold it for a major loss.

My point is, the stock market is not a guaranteed paycheck, but by refusing to invest, or by investing unwisely, you may also be risking your financial future. You can invest wisely in the market and in your own small business at the same time.

Corporate Misconduct

Corporate scandals have contributed greatly to economic uncertainty in this country. Whether companies have restated earnings or fabricated profits, greed has all too frequently overridden ethics, even in some of the nation's leading corporate headquarters. Hopefully the Enrons and the Tycos of our corporate landscape are a thing of the past. Here were two prime examples where greed cost employees of these scandal-ridden companies their jobs *and* their life savings.

It's my belief that corporate misconduct spurred a lot of people to consider owning a small business. Owning a business gives you a greater sense of control over your own destiny. Plus, you can *trust* company management when it's you.

Corporate scandals can also be great learning opportunities for business owners because our employees look to us as the CEO and watch how we conduct our business. It's imperative that we don't cut corners and that we do everything the right way one hundred percent of the time. Really, what is the difference between a CEO of a large company billing the company for millions and a CEO of a small company overdrawing his or her own business and then missing tax payments? Both actions are irresponsible and unethical.

Interest Rate Volatility

We are in a rising interest rate environment. Naturally, this makes investing in one's own business a more challenging prospect because the cost of borrowing is higher, and rising. Certainly, in a low interest rate environment, small businesses are able to take advantage and borrow money at more attractive rates. This was the case a few years back. Many people were also taking that opportunity to purchase homes or refinance their mortgages.

Now, times are different. But I would still contend it's never the wrong time to start your own business and start building equity. You may not be able to borrow as much as you were hoping to, but I think this financial hurdle forces you to more carefully consider your cash flow, watch your expenses, and keep tighter controls on your business in general. In the long run, this will teach you how to run a more efficient business.

Also, keep in mind that you can always restructure debt. And interest rates are cyclical – they may be rising now, but at some point they will fall again.

Social Security

The government designed Social Security to supplement workers' retirement funds. Unfortunately, for many, it's their *only* source of income in retirement. When the program began, there were approximately thirty workers for every individual needing Social Security. Today, that number has dropped to single digits. Consequently, as fewer workers support a continuously aging population, the impact on Social Security is devastating. Who knows what is going to happen in the next twenty to thirty years, but don't count on it being there for you when you retire.

Therefore, I think people who will be retiring within the next fifteen to twenty years would be wise to create a small business that will sustain them through their retirement years. Since Social Security is all many people have in retirement (or contributes the majority of their post-retirement income), alternative plans are critical.

Where To Start?

Local communities are abundant in free resources that will help educate you on topics such as wealth creation and running a small business. Once, while visiting Charlotte, North Carolina, I attended a presentation advertised in the local newspaper's Sunday business section. This free seminar, held in the public library, focused on entrepreneurship and was incredibly informative

If you are serious about becoming a Wealthy Entrepreneur, you should consider free seminars and courses, along with your research, part of your due diligence. They may also provide you with great networking opportunities.

You should also find your local Chamber of Commerce, Small Business Development Center,

SCORE Office, or Urban League and get involved. These organizations provide excellent contacts and offer many free resources.

Finally, churches today stress economic empowerment and many are creating development companies or are training their members on financial literacy. You may want to check with your church to see if they are providing this type of direction to members.

Let's Get Started

It doesn't matter if you have a lot of money or a little, your money is *your money*. It is important to you and that's all that matters. There have been many small businesses and fortunes created with as little as fifty dollars, and yours could be next!

In his book, *The Millionaire Mind*, Dr. Thomas J. Stanley notes that thirty-two percent of the millionaires he interviewed were entrepreneurs or business owners. Sixty-one percent created their wealth in one generation, meaning they received no inherited wealth. I love these two statistics because they tell me – and hopefully convince you – that you can create an abundance of wealth in your lifetime and you can do it through business ownership.

People create wealth in this country through ownership, and a business is an outstanding vehicle that can propel you to riches greater than you thought possible. I encourage all of my friends to own a business. I own my businesses (restaurants, real estate, and consulting practices) to help provide my children with options, and to continue to see life as full of possibilities.

In my presentations, I tell the story of my middle child who, at age five, approached me and said he planned to own thirty of my competitor's restaurants when he "got big." It later dawned on me what his declaration had really meant – that he could *visualize* himself owning a sixty million dollar business. *That's* economic empowerment!

Let's work together to help *your* children or loved ones see the possibilities in this world. Let's help give them the options that have so often eluded people in the past simply because they didn't think they were possible.

Check Your Financial Motivation and Set "SMART" Goals

In order to become a Wealthy Entrepreneur, you have to have strong financial motivation and the dedication to save your money. When I was saving money for my business, I used Paul Meyer's well-known goal-setting technique that I'd like to share with you. Its premise is that all goals should be SMART:

- ✓ Specific
- ✓ Measurable
- ✓ Accountable
- ✓ Realistic
- ✓ Timely

For example, if you have a goal to save $3,000,

be SMART about it. Write your goals in a way that incorporates all five components, i.e. *My savings will increase by $3,000 as of September 30, 2006 if I reduce my entertainment expenses from $200 to $100 each month.* This statement is Specific and Measurable, laying out a detailed plan that you can track. It is also Accountable and Realistic. Reducing something as simple as entertainment costs is both manageable and relatively easy. Cutting entertainment costs is also easy to track. Finally, this statement is timely. It sets a specific, realistic date.

Many people *talk* about their financial aspirations. But when you're serious about your goals, you write them down. You set dates for accomplishment. You review your goals regularly to keep yourself on schedule. Often, just by reviewing your goals and holding yourself accountable, you can eliminate behaviors that may prevent you from reaching those goals.

When you consider your financial motivation for owning your own business, dig deep and question if your chosen investment vehicle will sustain you through the tough periods. Owning a business is like a long run in the sand: It lasts longer and requires more effort than the typical run, so you need to be smart, pace yourself, and use the right tactics to meet the goal.

Many Wealthy Entrepreneurs have a passion for their business that is much greater than just the desire to make money, create wealth, or be the boss. Henry Ford, for example, wanted to make cars that were affordable for the masses. Yes, accomplishing this goal made him wealthy, but his desire to help the common person was what fueled and sustained his passion to become successful.

I started my consulting business because I wanted to help families enrich their lives through entrepreneurship the way my family has been blessed. More specifically, I want to impact the lives of children, particularly children who haven't been given the opportunity to see possibilities for their own future success. As part of my commitment, I donate a percentage of my earnings to charitable organizations like the local YMCA, the Ronald McDonald House, and the Black Achievers program.

~Personal Reflection~

Who's on your financial team?

I'm a big believer in having a strong financial team. That includes my accountant, my financial advisor, and my lawyer. You have to have at least one or two people you trust, with whom you can share your vision, who can give you a road map on how to get there, and, even more importantly, protect you and your family along the way.

I recently read a story where a young lady was praying for a repeal of the estate tax. Once her grandmother dies, this woman will be forced to sell assets to pay her grandparents' estate tax bill. This is a problem that could have been avoided with proper planning and a great financial team.

I personally can't understand the business owner who typically works sixty to eighty hours per week, dedicates his or her life to build a business, and then leaves it up to chance when it comes to estate planning because he or she doesn't want to pay a fee to the experts.

We hire experts in human resources, marketing, and strategic planning; why not hire experts in our financial affairs? Hire a great financial team, have them meet with you collectively at least once a year, and review your plan to make sure you are protecting your family and your number one financial asset, your business!

Where will you take your family on vacation in five years?

Visualize the vacation destination you'd most like to visit. How much money would it take to get there? You might even cut out a picture of the place and stick it on the wall. Then make a plan, and make your family part of that plan. In this way, everyone will be able to see the great benefits that come from making some sacrifices.

Today, my wife and I utilize vacations as motivation. When I started my consulting business, my wife had a few words of advice for me: "Make it worth our while!" With three young kids and my travel schedule, I make a lot of sacrifices to keep things running smoothly. And my wife sacrifices more than I do. As a result, we take a vacation each quarter, just the two of us, to energize our bodies and our relationship. These three to five day mini trips have been excellent and I would encourage you to do the same with your spouse or partner.

Where do you see yourself in ten years?

Visualize how big your business will be and the house you're going to live in. If you're going into debt to purchase a business, what's the plan for that debt once it's retired? How are you then going to invest that monthly payment? I know what I did once my restaurant was paid for – I put that money in an investment account. Forget about new cars or fancy jewelry, I wanted to put that money to work!

What will your net worth be at retirement?

This should really be a stretch goal, and you may find yourself adjusting it even higher with compounding interest and anything else that goes in your favor. (But you may also need to adjust lower.)

RESPECT YOUR BODY AND FIND BALANCE IN YOUR LIFE

"The first wealth is health."
Ralph Waldo Emerson, "Power,"
The Conduct of Life (1860)

If you don't have your health, what do you really have? In the early part of my career, I gained a modest six pounds in ten years. From the time I started the McDonald's® training program to the time I arrived in Lexington, I gained another *forty* pounds. I vividly recall the warning I received from my new doctor in Lexington: "Phil, your work schedule and your lifestyle are not compatible with life."

That statement really jolted me, and it sticks with me to this day. Here I was, throwing my heart and soul into this business in order to create a bright future for my family. But because I wasn't taking care of myself physically, there was a chance I wasn't going to be part of that future!

Soon after that doctor visit, I joined the local YMCA and started a workout routine, which included Krav Maga, a vigorous self-defense course. I now leave my cell phone at home when I go to exercise because this is my time to escape. I'm still working toward my weight goal, but I've lost twenty-eight pounds and shed a cholesterol problem in the process.

I'm now convinced that physical conditioning plays a large role in an entrepreneur's success. If you're working long hours, you need great stamina. I also find that when I'm physically fit I get fewer colds and I feel more energetic. And, if I want or need to, I can work longer without getting physically drained.

As a Wealthy Entrepreneur, I set my own hours. However, I work long hours not because I have to, but because I want to. My average day starts at around 6:00 a.m., and although I may not be working in the restaurants at that time, I'm thinking about my business or some business opportunity. When I'm in town, I take my son to school every morning. This is my special bonding time with him, and since I'm up and dressed, I go directly from the school to the gym to work out. I have created a system for bonding with my son and for maintaining my health.

I then eat breakfast and am on my way to one of

my restaurants, a meeting, or my office by 9:30 a.m. I'm usually home by 6:00 p.m. to spend time with my wife and kids until the kids' bedtime, around 9:00 p.m. I reserve late evenings for time-consuming activities like writing this book or rehearsing a speech. My day ends at around 10:30 p.m. If I didn't have the stamina and health, in addition to the love for what I do, I couldn't keep up this pace.

Today, my philosophy is balance. It's okay to treat yourself occasionally, but you have to know when it's time to get back on track.

I also now encourage everyone to exercise daily and visit a doctor for an annual physical. My family is young. And I owe it to myself, my wife, and my kids to take care of myself. And you owe it to yourself and your family too.

Keep in mind that as your business grows and you add employees, your insurance coverage and costs may be driven up by your employees' ages and other risk factors. Many of these risk factors can be reduced or eliminated by a balanced diet and exercise, so advocating a healthy lifestyle in the office will not only ensure a happy, healthy staff, but may also save you money in the long run.

I am also a big believer in systems and in keeping things simple. One of the best systems I have created for myself is the following: 20:1:2. What does this mean?

The 20 stands for 20 minutes of personal reflection each day. You will be amazed at what you can accomplish by planning or visualizing your goals for 20 minutes every single day. By finding a quiet space to think, plan, dream, or pray, everyday can easily turn your business and your life around.

Next, the number 1 stands for the number of hours of vigorous exercise I attempt to have in a day. Because I believe it is so important to put your money where you mouth is, I recently hired a personal trainer to put me through an intense workout two times per week, and I force myself to get out of bed and work out on my own the other days of the week. The energy and confidence I gain from my workouts is tremendous, and I believe is a catalyst for my success.

Finally, the number 2 represents the number of hours I give to my family in uninterrupted time each evening. When I enter the house, my cell phone is off and I am theirs until the kids go to bed, which is normally around 9:00. My goal each day is to give my family a minimum of two hours of my attention by focusing on each person individually.

This simple formula has helped me strengthen my faith and improve my performance. It has also improved my health and my relationship with my wife and kids. Give it a try for a month and send me an email at phil@philwilkins.com with your results.

onsider some of the side benefits of getting in shape. By working out consistently, I've been able to use the gym as a networking site. I recently met a manager from an insurance firm who arranged a speaking engagement for me. Ultimately, I was able to use a portion of the profits from this engagement to pay my gym membership for an entire year! I enjoy meeting people, and while I clearly don't expect every encounter to "pay off," I never know. I enjoy using the gym as a place to both exercise and meet people. However, it may not be for you. If you love golf or tennis, join a club and use these activities not only to improve your health but also to improve your business.

~Personal Reflection~

When was your last physical exam?

If you're thinking about leaving your position, get a physical *now*, before you leave the job and it becomes more difficult to do so. I hadn't had a physical exam in five years before I went to see the doctor who gave me that harsh warning. I just wasn't keeping track of that part of my life, and there was really no excuse for it. Now I get a physical every June, a requirement for participating in my sons' summer basketball camp. And I keep working out to make sure I'll be able to run up and down the court with those kids!

Is there a physical activity you and your spouse/partner can do together?

The typical business owner works approximately sixty hours a week. Think about the sacrifices you make working that many hours, and the lack of time you have left over for a spouse or loved one you miss. If there's an activity you can do together, it's a big plus. It keeps you both in shape, reduces stress, and gives you one-on-one time to talk.

What time is best for exercise?

The key is to schedule specific exercise time. Make it part of your daily routine. Personally, I like to work out in the morning because there are too many reasons for me *not* to do it in the evening, such as helping with my kids' homework, giving my wife a hand, etc. What time of day works best for you? Reserve it for your workout and stick to it.

STRATEGY 4

BLESSED OR STRESSED? MAINTAIN YOUR EMOTIONAL AND SPIRITUAL HEALTH!

Becoming an entrepreneur is a mental challenge, an emotional roller coaster, and in my experience, a real test of your faith. You've invested your heart, soul, and hard-earned cash and when things don't go as planned, it's difficult to stay focused and not lose your composure.

I vividly recall saying to myself over and over, "God didn't put you in this position to fail." It wasn't "chance" that I read that McDonald's® article. It wasn't chance that I sacrificed and pursued the dream of owning my own business for six years. That is purposeful direction and it didn't come by accident.

My first thirty days as a business owner were trying, to say the least, and I found myself constantly repeating my mantra. It was the middle of a hot, humid summer and the store's air conditioners weren't working consistently. I needed all the help I could get because we were running a big store promotion (ninety-nine-cent triple cheeseburgers) and three employees walked out in the middle of their shifts, complaining of the heat. When one of those employees later returned to find he no longer had a job, he set a trash container on fire. Another employee tried to make a pass at a customer, which then brought the customer's boyfriend into the store looking for justice.

During all of this drama, I do remember asking myself, "What in the hell have I done?" But then I went back to my faith and realized that I wasn't put here to fail. You'll have these moments too. This is the time to stay focused. Review your business plan, review your goals, and keep your faith. Trust me, things will improve!

When I first started my business, I routinely tried to think up systems in order to alleviate my stress. For instance, I instituted a weekly managers' meeting, when managers reported to me on operations, labor, and food costs. I no longer had to worry about collecting all that information myself. And the weekly meeting had the added benefit of shifting ownership of performance from me to my managers and getting them more involved and invested in the business.

As you begin your business, think of systems that you can put in place to help your operation run more efficiently and help you reduce stress.

Visualization is an important part of goal-setting. Try creating a poster board with pictures of your goals or a scrapbook with visual and written images of your aspirations. Look at those images once a week and see yourself succeeding. Try it, it works!

~Personal Reflection~

Do you recognize your signs of stress?

When I am stressed, I eat and I end up gaining weight. It's important to recognize your stress symptoms and what causes them, because it helps you figure out how to alleviate your anxiety.

How does your spouse/partner react to you when you're stressed?

I'm a different person when I'm stressed. My wife just leaves me alone at these times and lets me work things out for myself. This works for us, and may for others too. But if your system for coping with stress doesn't work, you need look for ways to make a change, whether that's altering your behavior, counseling, or another tactic. You need to fight for your family and do whatever it takes to keep things at home on track while you're building your business.

What time of day do you have to yourself?

Everyone needs some down time. Find a way to make personal time and space for yourself. In our house, my wife has a sitting area where she likes to go relax after the kids go to bed, with her TV, her sofa, and her pictures on the wall. My quiet space in the house? I'm relegated to the basement!

What time of day are you most energized and motivated?

Some people are most creative and productive late at night. For me, early morning is when I'm most alert and energized; however, due to my busy schedule, I'm often forced to do a chunk of work at night. Figure out what time is your best time, and use it to tackle the tough issues.

STRATEGY 5

Work Your Skills, Hire Your Weaknesses!

Although I now do it for a living, I used to have a great fear of public speaking. I even received a C in my college public speaking course. It wasn't until the company I previously worked for offered "Toastmasters," a public speaking workshop, that I became more comfortable with speaking in public.

I mention this because prior to owning my own businesses, I was in sales. I needed to overcome my fear of speaking in public if I was going to be successful. "Toastmasters" was an excellent opportunity for me to strengthen a skill that was a weakness for me.

Now is the time to determine your strengths and which skills you may need to improve. Skill assessment requires a lot of honesty and courage. Seek input from family, friends, and even your boss.

The key is for you to get honest feedback so you can accurately assess your abilities. Even if you decide not to pursue entrepreneurship, at the very least you will become a better employee with more marketable skills.

As you build your team, look for employees or partners whose skills and expertise *complement* yours and fill in the skill or knowledge areas you may lack.

The talents and expertise of my management team complement mine. I am the visionary and I enjoy building the business through networking and meeting different people. My business manager is detail-oriented when it comes to numbers and policies, and superb at planning themes for meetings and creating employee incentives. My director of operations is very technical and procedure-oriented, has excellent communication skills, and is great with a computer, something I am not.

In small business, many people make the mistake of hiring people with the *same* skills as theirs. Don't make that mistake! Before I hired my two senior managers, I spent several hours interviewing each of them, trying to make sure our skill sets were compatible. To do this, I had to know what my weaknesses were in order to look for these strengths in others. If I'd hired another salesperson to help me run my business, I guarantee you I'd be on "credit hold" after ninety days because neither of us would want to pay the bills!

Once you have assembled your team, give them direction, put your follow-up systems in place, and get out of their way. There are times when I feel like jumping in during a managers' meeting and saying something, but then I realize I would be adding confusion instead of helping.

It *is* hard for many entrepreneurs to let go. Your business is your baby and you are in business to be the boss. But I, for one, am more concerned with making money than with maintaining my image as "the boss." In my company, everyone knows the boss is my business manager, not me!

I pay these professionals to *run* my business. My role is to *grow* other businesses. When you find people who are capable, *let* them take over. This revelation will gain you the freedom so many people desire.

Some skills I think are necessary to be a Wealthy Entrepreneur include:

✓ **Communication** – the ability to listen, understand what people are saying, and respond appropriately.

When you mention communication skills, everyone immediately thinks of your ability to speak. But listening is often *more* important. We tell our managers that when a customer returns an item, they should hold their tongue, listen, empathize, and fix the problem quickly.

As an owner, you may find your employees sometimes feel intimidated by you and give you information they think you want to hear versus the real deal. If you are not willing to listen calmly, people may hesitate to tell you what you need to know.

You can learn so much more about your business just by listening! Momma used to tell me you have two ears and one mouth for a reason. Now I know why.

✓ **Respect** – the ability to respect other people's feelings, efforts, and opinions.

When I moved from Cincinnati to Lexington, it took me a while to figure out how to communicate with people. I was too abrupt, too direct. In Lexington, things are handled more slowly, more diplomatically. I thought my way of doing things was more efficient, but I wasn't in Cincinnati anymore. I had to learn how to do business in Lexington. It taught me a valuable lesson about respecting differences and showed me that different situations and environments call for different approaches.

✓ **Appreciation of Diversity** – the ability to work with a diverse group of people will only become more important as demographics in the United States continue to change.

Diversity is becoming a larger issue in this country every day. The minority population will grow dramatically over the next forty-five years and it will change how American businesses operate. There is also a lot of untapped business within diverse markets. Don't take my word for it, look at what Magic Johnson has been able to accomplish with his businesses. He saw a market in neglected, minority communities. By working with established franchises, he was able to build movie theaters and restaurants that now generate huge profits.

I have been to Magic's headquarters in California and have visited his Friday's® in Crenshaw. True, Magic has leverage that few others have. But he shows us that the dollars are out there. People in communities such as Harlem, Oakland, and Gary want and need places to eat and shop and are willing to spend the money if the business is well-run and respectful.

✓ **Financial Literacy** – a solid understanding of how your business generates and uses its cash.

Financial literacy is a crucial element of business success. Even though I have a business manager who has a great understanding of accounting and an accountant working on my business, I still read books to strengthen my financial knowledge.

Having a clear understanding of your numbers and how your business compares to others in your industry is critical. Equally critical is having your financial information up to date. I can't understand business owners who don't have regular income statements produced and reviewed by an accountant. How can you fix a problem you don't know you have? Small businesses should have their numbers reviewed monthly, quarterly, or at least annually. Whatever time frame you choose, review your numbers regularly to spot potential problems early.

ere is a prime example of why it is important to hire people who complement your strengths and weaknesses and then step aside and allow them to do their jobs:

For two weeks, I let a loan application sit on my desk because I hate doing paperwork, even though I knew it would save us money in the long run. After kicking myself for procrastinating, I finally decided to fill out the forms and send them in to the bank.

My business manager had prepared all of our financial documentation, placed a check inside the packet, and had everything ready to send overnight to the bank. I completed the paperwork, and in the process, pulled everything out of the packet. As I finished the task, I put the materials back into the envelope with the exception of the financial documentation, which I filed away in my home office. I left out the information that was most important! Why? Because it's not my strength.

Not only did I waste hours doing a project that would have been much better handled by my business manager, but as a result I was late to my son's basketball practice and my wife, nine months pregnant at the time, wasn't pleased. Anyone who has lived with a pregnant woman knows to keep her happy!

Needless to say, I will never complete another loan application for as long I own this business and have my business manager.

~Personal Reflection~

How will your strengths enhance your performance as a small business owner?

In my organization, I know my role: I'm the visionary and the motivator. My business and operations managers are the "go-to" guys. They know how to take my ideas and make them work. We are successful because our work arrangement plays to all of our strengths.

How will your weaknesses make it more difficult for you to run your business?

I used to think my strength would be back office administration because when I was preparing to become a business owner, I kept my personal financial house in order. But I found that once I owned the business, I wanted to focus on the stores and not get bogged down by paperwork, so I put it off. I had to recognize my growing administrative weakness and bring in people who were strong in that area and could help keep my business running smoothly.

How well do you prioritize?

Prioritizing is an important skill for any business owner. In my businesses, I focus on the things that make money! I follow up with clients, make calls, work on proposals, and then delegate any task such as completing forms and invoicing and letters to the assistant or my business manager. Whatever I can delegate, I try to move to other people so that I can concentrate on what makes the bank account grow!

Are you comfortable working with a diverse group of people?

Depending on what type of business you're entering, you will probably need to be aware of demographic trends and sensitive to cultural differences in the workplace. For instance, there were no Hispanic employees in my Cincinnati store, but in Lexington, over forty percent of my staff is Hispanic. Cultural awareness and sensitivity is also very important in your relationships with customers and vendors.

STRATEGY 6

RESPECT AND INCLUDE YOUR SPOUSE/PARTNER

When you go through a major transition, like becoming a new parent, starting a new job, or becoming a business owner, it impacts everyone close to you in some way. It might be positive; if your spouse or partner's skills complement yours, owning a business gives you an opportunity to build something together.

On the other hand, a major transition will probably add significant stress that can fracture an otherwise healthy relationship. The key is to discuss and resolve issues *now*, rather than wait until you're further into your new venture. Your time is often not your own when you build a business, so it's important to handle issues that will impact your family or loved ones before you start.

During my transition to business ownership, I was still traveling for my "day job" during the week, had a full-weekend commitment at McDonald's®, and my wife was about to give birth to our first child. All these factors caused great stress for my wife, who was also working full time.

I was busy chasing my dream, so it wasn't until much later that I could see the impact my aspirations had on my relationship with my wife. During the early days of the transition, she would tell me she was lonely. That's quite common among spouses of self-employed people. Long days are not uncommon. But they shouldn't be the goal.

My dream was to be self-employed; my wife's dream was for her husband to be with his family. Initially, there was conflict. Today, we enjoy the benefits of self-employment, including flexibility, freedom, and control. But this only happened because of an attitude shift on my part, i.e. that my business should work for *me*, and not the other way around.

Although my wife is not actively involved in the day-to-day management of the business, she adds great value. For instance, she created the name "M.A.C. Days," or Managers Appreciating Crew. Each M.A.C. Day, the crew picks a job for the managers to do (whether unpleasant like cleaning the bathroom, or funny like making the managers wear ridiculous hats and greeting customers during the "Derby" week). The whole staff loves these events and I'm grateful to my wife for coming up with them.

I think it's important to find ways to involve your spouse or loved one in your business, even if it's not in day-to-day operations. I know that if anything were to happen to me, my wife is more than capable of taking over the business because of the many discussions we've had and the core management we've put in place.

Business ownership has been a blessing for me and has also had a positive impact on my relationships with my children. I recommend exposing your children to your business because it not only allows them to spend time with you and understand your job, but it may help them develop their own business sense. When we opened a new store, my sons, at the ages of six and three, were crawling under the tables to clean spots that the managers couldn't reach.

Now, my oldest child is learning how to read my reports and my middle child sits on my lap when I check our sales. They are fascinated by all of it and want to learn more about business. I often take them in to the office with me. They're excited (probably in large part because we have candy in the office), but I want them to get a feel for the pace of business and be exposed to as much as possible.

~Personal Reflection~

***What sacrifices will you and your spouse/
partner make to reach your objectives?***

For us, the sacrifices were pretty major. We
had a beat-up gray Ford Explorer with faulty
air conditioning and a broken armrest for the
longest time. I had managers who drove nicer
cars than we did! Some would not be willing
to delay material gratification to that extent,
but to get into business for yourself, you may
have to do just that.

***If your spouse/partner will be involved, how
will you communicate?***

This is an important question, particularly
if you have employees. You shouldn't be
calling each other "honey" or "babe" in the
workplace. And you shouldn't let employees
see you argue. You need to establish a
hierarchy with clearly defined roles. My
biggest challenge would be how to forget
about that hierarchy when the day's over and
you are at home. Talk about these things up
front.

How will you separate home from work?

If I'm on the cell phone discussing business, I'll drive around the neighborhood for a while rather than walk into the house on the phone.

And, I turn off the cell phone once I'm in the house – anyone who really needs to reach me knows the home phone number. I find I do often talk about business with my wife when I'm home, but I try to put limits on these conversations and make time to just be a family. When you're home, be home.

What does your spouse/partner expect from you?

You have to figure out what you both want and what you both expect of each other. As I've said, there's my dream, and then there's my wife's dream. We try to be supportive of each other, and my wife knows when to gently chide me. She'll say, "Phil, I love your ambition. Just make sure you don't miss the important things."

STRATEGY 7

IT'S ALL ABOUT THE DEAL – SO DO YOUR HOMEWORK

The process of analyzing a business opportunity and putting the deal together is really where you begin to make your money. Why do I say this? Because the better the deal you negotiate up front, the sooner and more effectively you can start to build your wealth.

Make sure you understand all the details of the deal and the ins and outs of the business – you need to feel confident that after you sign, you'll be able to make the business work and make ends meet. I remember when I was buying one of my stores, I thought the seller's sales projections were a bit high. We went back, renegotiated, and I ultimately got a $50,000 concession on the selling price. That's not a lot of money, but it was still $50,000 more in my pocket. And that's crucial, because this is where you begin to build your wealth.

So before you put your money on the table, you need to dig in and do the necessary research. With thorough due diligence, you make well-informed decisions. The Wealthy Entrepreneur uses all available resources in this process, such as the local Chamber of Commerce, Small Business Development Centers, and the Internet to gain as much information as possible about a new opportunity.

The due diligence phase is the time to familiarize yourself with the five C's of credit:

- ✓ **Character:** Do you pay your bills on time?
- ✓ **Cash Flow:** Will your business idea generate enough cash flow to service the debt and provide excess cash to run the business and live on?
- ✓ **Collateral:** Will your new business have enough assets to cover the loan or do you personally have enough assets?
- ✓ **Capitalization:** What resources does the company have, such as assets, equity, and retained earnings, as well as money you've invested?
- ✓ **Conditions:** What external issues could impact operations? Government regulations? Industry and market trends?

Financial institutions examine all of these factors when deciding whether or not to lend you money.

If, for example, you're habitually late paying bills, the bank views it as a "character" issue. Therefore, knowing what criteria financial institutions look for will help you better prepare for a career as an entrepreneur. You need to be able to honestly examine your personal history to determine if your opportunity is feasible and realistic.

When I buy a new restaurant, my financial team and I scrutinize the projections. We input every line item and every expense we can think of to determine if the deal is any good. We analyze how the business is currently performing, and we keep our estimates conservative.

My assumption is that the business will take time to turn. If the business is underperforming, it will take a while to analyze whatever is bringing it down and take corrective action. Be realistic – I never let my ego get in the way and convince me that I can turn a business around overnight. If you can make money on a deal in the worst-case scenario, then it is probably a good deal. Presumably, things will only improve from there.

With an existing business, I want to see the last three to five years of profit and loss statements (P&L's), customer counts, and average transaction amounts. These are the hot buttons in our industry; from here I can see trends and determine if the business is underperforming or maximizing its returns. I also want to see five years of sales history, recent re-investments, and three years of tax returns. The P&L's may be outstanding, but that may mean the seller is maximizing profitability by shifting expenses from one business to another, to make this business appear healthier than it is. Don't trust the people you're buying businesses from. Your job is to protect the assets of your family. Do your homework thoroughly before making any deal.

~Personal Reflection~

What is the one thing I should know before executing this deal?

There is no "one thing" to know, there are *many things* to know. The more you know about the industry and the business you're getting into, the better positioned you are to negotiate your deal. And the better deal you negotiate up front, the more money you'll make in the long term. As one friend and fellow business owner put it to me, "It's all about the deal."

STRATEGY 8

BE REAL ABOUT YOUR FINANCES

Today, "financial literacy" is a very popular term. As Wealthy Entrepreneurs, we *must* understand our finances and be aware of how our businesses make money.

I have found that in my business, I need to be as strategic about growth as I am about managing cash during slow periods. Many business owners make the mistake of growing too big too fast without the systems and financial reserves in place to cover a downturn in volume. Be cautious about your growth.

To the small business owner, one bad deal or bad investment can eliminate cash flow or reserves quickly and subsequently pull the business down. Therefore, in my seminars, I discuss making investments and the tests that must be met prior to investing.

If my business is investing in a piece of equipment or a product, it must drive sales or reduce expenditures. One thing I also try to do is keep my profit margins in mind. What do I mean by this? If a piece of equipment costs $10,000, and my margins are ten percent, will this product drive $100,000 of new sales or savings? If not, then I may or may not invest. Even if I do invest, I need to have at least considered the financial impact of the investment on my cash flow and on my cash reserves.

As a new business owner, especially if you're coming from corporate America, you will be tempted to spend money on anything that needs repair or you feel you need. My suggestion would be to first try to fix things yourself, analyze how and why the equipment broke initially, and before you make a purchase, keep your margins in mind.

Personal Due Diligence

Are you on top of your own financials? Do you know where your money is going? You should get a handle on your personal budget before you consider any new business venture.

Consider your mortgage, your utility bills, your grocery bills – all the weekly and monthly costs of running your household. Can you find ways to eliminate or reduce any of these items? Remember the line from my old corporate job that I mentioned for Strategy 1? "Keep your options open and your payments low." These are words to *live* by when you're starting your own business. Figure out what costs you can cut or get rid of, and keep looking *back* at your budget to see where you can cut some more!

The Income/Expense statement is a great tool to help you do this. It allows you to track your personal expenses and figure out if your household is running a fiscally responsible budget. You should make multiple copies of this statement so you can track your progress monthly and annually.

You can download full-size versions of the worksheets in this book from my website, www.philwilkins.com.

Sample Income/Expense statement:

Item	Month Total	Annual Total
Income:		
Salary*		
Spouse Salary*		
Dividend Income		
Rental Income		
Other Income		
Total Income		
Expenses:		
Automobile(s)		
Bank Charges		
Child Care		
Clothing		
Credit Cards		
Dry Cleaning		
Education		
Entertainment		
Groceries		
Hair Care		
Home Repair		
Household misc.		
Insurance		
Medical		
Mortgage		
Membership(s)		
Utilities: Telephone		
Water		
Electric		
Gas		
Cable TV		
Misc. Expense		
Total Expenses		
Net Income **		

*Salary = Take home pay or net pay after taxes and withdrawals

**Net income = total income minus total expenses

As you examine and analyze your own financials, gather and set aside the documents you will need to obtain financing for your new business. You should have the following documents ready and available to show to bankers or investors:

- ✓ Three years of tax returns,
- ✓ Three years of bank statements,
- ✓ Deed to your home,
- ✓ W-2's for the past year,
- ✓ Two to six months of investment account statements.

I needed all these documents within seven to fourteen days for my McDonald's® loan applications. Would you be able to access all of these documents that quickly? Make sure you have them at your fingertips, and make sure they're stored in a safe place.

Do you understand the tax implications of your actions? For example, you may want to sell stock or use your 401k to begin your venture. Such actions could ultimately result in a tax hit you weren't expecting. Speak to your accountant and make sure you understand any potential tax liability.

Finally, consider your personal credit record. Many services now provide you with free credit reports. If yours needs work, consider these tips I found in an issue of *Smart Money* magazine and start incorporating them into your financial habits:

- ✓ Don't pay late or go bankrupt.

- ✓ Don't use all your available credit.
- ✓ Limit your number of credit cards. You should have one to three, maximum.
- ✓ Avoid inquiries. For example, accepting a "ten percent off" store credit card generates a credit inquiry which tends to make lenders nervous.

~Personal Reflection~

Can you build your business and keep your current job? If so, how will you allocate your time and efforts?

You really need drive, ambition, and perseverance to make it all work, particularly if you're juggling your current job with starting a new business. The key is to block out time for each of your activities.

Are you willing to take a cut in pay or withstand pay fluctuations?

This is an especially important question if you're starting a business from scratch. If you have to take a cut in pay to start your business (and you probably will), decide what amount of money you need to live on, and how long you could go with no salary. I took a seventy percent pay cut to start working for myself.

But I was paying down my debt, making ends meet, and I knew I wouldn't stay at that salary level forever. To me, the sacrifice was well worth it.

How much money will you need to get your business started and to stay afloat?

Look at your projections. Know your break-even number and decide whether it's realistic for you and your goals. Know your monthly expenses – mortgage, groceries, etc. Can your business support these monthly expenses? Take a long, hard look at these numbers before you leap!

How do you currently track your spending?

I strongly suggest getting a personal financial computer program, like Quicken, to organize your personal finances.

Initial Investment Worksheet

This is something I wish I'd had when I was waiting for my first business opportunity to become available. When my opportunity arrived, I spent two weeks scrambling to prepare. I spent *a lot* of money – some of which I hadn't been prepared for. I hadn't thought about the utility deposit or training expenses. If you're tight on cash to begin with, these smaller expenses can really add up.

Now when I'm considering a new opportunity, I use a chart such as the example below to help me anticipate my start-up costs:

Category	Item	Estimated Cost	When Due	To Whom
Land and Improvements				
Rent/Security Deposit				
Grand-Opening Expenses				
Training				
Utilities Deposit				
Insurance				
Accounting				
Legal				
Licenses				
Equipment				
Inventory				
Working Capital (3 months)				
Tax Liability (project with accountant)				
Marketing and Advertising				

STRATEGY 9

Know Your Business!

When I evaluate an existing business or industry, I am thorough. First, I want to understand *why* the person is selling the business, so I try to enlist as many people with expertise as I can find to help me gather information. I'll call a real estate broker to ask what's going on in the area. Maybe a competitor has signed a lease on a parcel next to the business I'm considering. What do you think would potentially happen to the value of my business when the competitor opens? In business, the person with the most information often wins – so make sure that person is you.

Walk through the business. If you don't have the expertise, pay someone to evaluate the equipment, the structure of the building, etc., to make sure your investment is sound. Maintenance and repair on old, faulty equipment is not only costly, but may be an additional source of frustration for your employees. Buildings that leak can create a health hazard by promoting mold, cause unsightly stains on ceiling tiles, or promote decay of the structure.

I rejected my first restaurant initially because, in my estimation, it wasn't up to standards. If you find problems that will cost you money, those are negotiating points. If the business is being sold "as is," you need to factor the cost of repairs into your projections. This is why you need cash *reserves* so you can afford to reinvest in your business.

I try to interview as many people as possible during this stage of negotiation. If you're buying a franchise, you should get a list of current owners in the state or nationally. Call these people and ask them questions. If you're buying a manufacturing business, call customers and suppliers to determine their history. Customers can tell you if a business has been neglected or well-run.

If your business is a car wash, for example, set up meetings with car wash owners or managers in a different city and ask them questions. You'll be *amazed* at how much information you can gather just by letting someone else talk while you listen and take notes.

Who are the successful business owners in the industry you're exploring? Find those people, study them, and ask *them* questions. Here are some ideas for what to ask:

✓ What's made your business successful?

- ✓ How do you spend your time?
- ✓ How do you pay taxes? Payroll?
- ✓ What are your typical annual reinvestment needs and how do you plan for them?
- ✓ When do customers pay?
- ✓ When do suppliers expect payment?
- ✓ Does the business have seasonal swings? How do you survive slow periods?
- ✓ How does visibility/traffic flow impact your sales?
- ✓ What are your hours of operation and when are you busiest? Slowest?
- ✓ If you could change one thing about the industry, what would it be?
- ✓ What are your specific goals for the business?

I would also gather research on competitors. If you know how much the average customer spends there, you can easily determine your competition's sales during a certain time frame just by watching their customer flow. This will help you determine the health of your business opportunity.

Know the industry you're getting into. If the industry's been stagnant at two to three percent growth for several years, then projecting twenty percent annual growth is not realistic.

Industry trends are equally important to consider. Think about how cell phones have practically eliminated the need for the pay phone, or how those larger cars from the 1970s were replaced by smaller, more fuel-efficient cars. Industry changes can impact future cash flow and value of your business.

Finally, I always try to use current numbers in my projections to see if I can make money from the business as it's run today. I assume that I'm no better or worse off than the current owner, and I want my projections to be realistic and conservative.

~Personal Reflection~

What is the reputation of the industry/business you're considering?

Will you be happy and proud to work in this industry? The Gordon Gecko character from the movie *Wall Street* forever tainted the image of a stockbroker. Now we refer to brokers as financial advisors and planners.

Do existing customers and suppliers feel the business is well-run?

Go sit in the restaurant or shop the floor. Talk to customers. Ask the store manager what he or she thinks of the business. Find the suppliers and ask them questions.

If the business is new, what would make customers want to purchase your product or service? Have you done research to determine if customers want your product or service?

As a business owner, you need to know what differentiates your product or service from all the competitors' offerings. What's unique about your operations? Do you fill a currently unmet need?

Are there enough potential customers to cover your expenses, and is the market growing?

Make sure you've found a niche or market that's rich enough and deep enough to support your business.

STRATEGY 10

ASSEMBLE A TEAM OF FINANCIAL PROFESSIONALS

I think it's vitally important for a Wealthy Entrepreneur to surround himself or herself with trusted financial professionals. I rely on my financial team to help steer me through business opportunities, manage my existing businesses, and secure my family's financial well-being.

How do you choose the right advisors? In my experience, great advisors care about you and your family and do the right thing one hundred percent of the time. Here are some of my personal experiences with advisors who either earned my trust, or lost it:

I went looking for a new accountant when I became concerned that my previous one was not sharing enough information with me. After getting a referral from a colleague, I called to inquire whether there might be steps I could be taking before my new business opened. She quickly faxed me a five-page list of steps and told me I'd find them helpful, whether or not I needed her services. Needless to say, I hired her that day and have found her to be a great asset ever since.

It still burns me to think about one I fired when I was living in Cincinnati. I'd noticed a large amount of money missing from my 401K and called to ask him about it. Instead of helping me – he said he was "busy" – he gave me a customer service phone number. Four hours later, I'd managed to get my money back. I then fired my financial advisor on the spot! What good is an advisor if they don't provide you with a service?

When I moved to Lexington, I had my estate plan reviewed by an extremely bright young attorney, and my wife and I created a trust to protect our children in case something happened to us. Six months later, I met a financial advisor at a business function who offered me a complimentary review of my estate plan. (I didn't tell her I'd just had it done.) Because she works on commission, I was expecting her to come back with some suggestions. Imagine my surprise when she came back and said, "You're in good shape; I wouldn't change a thing. Whoever did your plan was very detailed. Your insurance is adequate for the current size of your estate." I really appreciated her honesty and long-term view, and I hired her that day.

Accounting Considerations

My accountant is a key member of my team. I have her review all my deals *before* I execute any contract or pay one dime. She bills a monthly fee for financial statements and a separate fee for personal and business income taxes. She also lets me call her whenever necessary at no additional charge. (I hate being nickel and dimed!)

The selection of an accountant is a personal decision. I would suggest interviewing several. You may find that your current tax advisor is not sophisticated enough to handle your new business needs. You need a great resource.

Are you familiar with the common financial ratios that are used today?

✓ **Net Debt**: Measures the amount of debt as a percentage of sales owed to outside creditors:

$$\frac{\text{Total Liabilities}}{\text{Total Liabilities + Capital}}$$

✓ **Quick Ratio**: Demonstrates what assets your business can immediately convert to cash:

$$\frac{\text{Cash + Marketable Securities + Account Receivables}}{\text{Current Liabilities}}$$

✓ **Inventory Turns**: The amount of times your inventory turns in a given month:

$$\frac{\text{Current Month COGS}}{\text{Average Inventory}}$$

✓ **Current Ratio**: Includes inventory and measures how quickly you can turn an asset to cash:

$$\frac{\text{Current Assets}}{\text{Current Liabilities}}$$

✓ **Net Cash Flow**: The amount of cash your business generates after everyone has been paid:

Operating Income + Depreciation - Debt Service = Cash Flow from Operations

$$
\begin{array}{rl}
 & \text{Cash Flow from Operations} \\
- & \text{Operators Draw} \\
- & \text{Administration Cost} \\
\hline
= & \text{Net Cash Flow}
\end{array}
$$

Many small business owners attempt to control expenses by using an accounting service on a quarterly or annual basis to reconcile their records. We've all read articles about business owners who have shortcut their expenses by eliminating the accountant. To me, that's putting your business and your family at risk.

In my business, my reports are done on a monthly basis and, ideally, are in my hands by the twentieth of the following month. As I mention throughout this book and in my seminars, Wealthy Entrepreneurs recognize that business is a team sport. What better teammate can you have than an accountant whose purpose is to help you make more money? I want my accountant reviewing my books regularly and providing suggestions for improvement. I also want someone who has experience in my industry and who can evaluate or even compare my business to another in my industry.

If you are like most business owners, you are out making calls, billing items, creating marketing strategies, and so on. You don't have time to follow up on every financial detail. It just makes good business sense to have a competent teammate you can rely on to be on top of these details.

Many accountants can provide payroll, bill paying, and other services to free you up so you can do what you do well – grow your business. These are value-added services, but you will have to determine if they will help you become more efficient at running your business. The services might be expensive, but they might also save you money, allow you to build your business faster, or protect you from an unexpected tax hit.

~Personal Reflection~

Have you compiled recommendations on each accountant you're considering?

As with any other service, check the references on any accountant you're considering. Remember, this person will be handling your confidential and sensitive documents. You want to make sure you can trust him or her with this information.

How frequently will you meet with your accountant?

Don't just wait until tax time. If you're running a business, you want to be strategizing and doing your tax planning throughout the year, in order to minimize your tax impact.

Does this accountant have experience in your industry to track normal spending and profitability?

I feel very comfortable knowing that my accountant understands my business well because she has other clients in this industry. She can give me perspective on how my business is doing in relation to others in the industry.

How accessible is your accountant?

Is your accountant available after hours, when you may be doing your paperwork? I try to reserve business hours for running and growing my business. The best time for me to speak to my accountant is in the evening. This was especially crucial when I was starting my business.

Legal Considerations

My attorneys are also important players on my team of experts. Selecting an attorney is a process that must be done with care. I would encourage you to get a couple of references from people you know and trust and be willing to pay for good legal advice.

It is better to pay money for great advice than waste money later on a frivolous lawsuit or a claim that could damage your family's future. Consequently, I use a number of attorneys that have different specialties in areas of interest to me.

For example, if I establish a new company, the attorney I use may be different than the one I use to establish my wills or trust. My rationale is that I want someone who is more knowledgeable about this topic than I, someone who can help me avoid potential pitfalls and who can help me find opportunities.

Your attorney can help you decide what type of legal structure best fits your needs:

✓ **Sole Proprietor**:
   Advantages: Simple; taxed at owner's personal tax level and only once.
   Disadvantages: Personal liability; limited deductions.

✓ **General Partnership**:
   Advantages: Multiple members; income flows through to owners based on percentage of ownership; all partners vote in management decisions.

Disadvantages: No limited liability; responsible for partners' actions.

✓ **Limited Partnership**:
Advantages: Multiple members; income flows through based on ownership percentages; limited liability for limited partners.
Disadvantages: No limited liability for general partners; general partners control business; limited partners have no authority.

✓ **S Corporations**:
Advantages: Limited liability; tax advantages.
Disadvantages: Limited number of shareholders (75 maximum).

✓ **C Corporation**:
Advantages: Limited personal liability; no limit to shareholders.
Disadvantages: Business deductions can't be used to reduce personal taxes; income is taxed at corporate level, then again in dividends.

✓ **Limited Liability Company**:
Advantages: Personal liability protection; pass income through unlimited shareholders.
Disadvantages: If more than one member, you will need an attorney to draft an operating agreement for you.

Many small businesses are sole proprietorships because of the ease, simplicity, and minimal cost. I am not a lawyer, and I am not telling you what to do, but I would never operate a sole proprietorship because of the personal liabilities.

I want my home and my business separate. You can come after me professionally if we make a mistake, but leave my home out of it. Consequently, I will make the investment and create a limited liability company or an S corporation, which provides protection and doesn't double tax.

Check with your legal advisor and also visit the Internal Revenue Service (IRS) website for additional information on each of the legal entities: www.irs.gov.

The IRS actually has a CD you can receive free of charge that discusses the different entities and provides instruction on which forms you need to use when completing your tax returns as a business owner.

~Personal Reflection~

Will your attorney review your employee handbook and benefits plan?

Your attorney can help make sure you're compliant with all laws concerning your benefits, plans, contracts, etc. Work with your lawyer to keep yourself out of trouble!

Is your attorney a specialist or does he/she have a general practice? Which one are you more comfortable with?

If you have an employment law issue, you don't need an estate attorney. Make sure you're selecting the attorney who is most familiar with the laws you're addressing. You get what you pay for!

STRATEGY 11

Don't Go Broke; Select a Workspace That Fits Your Budget!

Since I have a retail business, I did not initially need an office. It wasn't until we expanded to two stores that I began to consider having one. I don't entertain clients in my office, but it became important to me to have a central location where the back office staff could work that was also on a bus line for employees without their own transportation. In addition, the office became a space where we could invite managers and crew to meet.

As with your other business decisions, if you decide to open an office, be prudent about the costs. I was shocked by how expensive office furniture can be! I once found a nice desk that was clearly out of my price range. As my mouth fell open in surprise, the salesman, not knowing what I did for a living, asked me, "What's wrong – caviar tastes but a McDonald's® budget?"

"Exactly," I said. I didn't tell him about my McDonald's® stores until I was leaving the store empty handed. Guess whose mouth was open then?

An office can be a great sales tool, but it can also be a substantial cash drain. Carefully consider what the office will be used for, and use good taste and judgment when selecting furniture, colors, and decorations.

G ive a lot of thought to how much back office help you think you're going to need. In my experience, general and administrative expenses are easy to add and tough to remove. When you're considering hiring administrative assistants, buying or renting office space, or taking extra salary for yourself, proceed with caution!

~Personal Reflection~

Are there other professionals with whom you can share your office?

It may be advantageous to consider sharing staff, equipment, and space. You may find such an arrangement in an office suites setting. I currently own an office building that offers office suites and I wish I'd known about them when I started my business. In our building, we provide office furniture, secretarial support, copier, fax, an inviting reception area, and conference rooms. Many buildings like this one will also rent a virtual office for individuals who need a mailing address in a particular town. You may also be able to rent a conference room for a small fee. An office suite arrangement could save you a lot of money if you're starting a new venture.

What are the advantages/disadvantages of leasing your office vs. purchasing?

If you purchase the office, how will that affect your cash flow? When I purchased my office it was after one of my restaurants was paid for and the office building generated enough rental income to pay for itself.

However, coming up with capital for the down payment was carefully planned so that it wouldn't damage my cash flow.

What office equipment will you need?

There are phones, faxes, scanners, etc. to consider. These items can add up quickly. Know your technology – it can save you money!

Will the office drain your cash or save you money?

Be realistic and honest about your needs. Think about the role the office will play.

STRATEGY 12

UNDERSTAND YOUR INCOME STATEMENTS AND CASH FLOW

I once recommended a banker to a friend who was helping a non-profit to better understand and manage their finances. That got me thinking: How much do I really understand about my own business finances – balance sheets, P&L's, etc? At the time, I didn't know much! So I started asking more questions of my own advisors and reading anything I could on the subject. Don't be afraid to invest time and effort into reading books and consulting experts about the way things work. It will help you make better business decisions, and could save or earn you money in the long run.

Often when evaluating a business, we consider how much it's doing in sales without looking at the total picture. A business with strong sales may or may not be a wise investment; there are *many* factors in addition to sales that influence the profitability and cash flow of a business. Let's evaluate two businesses in the same industry and compare their income statements:

> John and Jane each own a health club. John's health club is fifteen years old and well established. His location is in a mature, middle-class neighborhood and he currently has 4,000 members who pay $30 in monthly dues. John's equipment is slightly older and his building will need renovations in the next few years. Because his staff is more seasoned, his manager makes $55,000 per year. John's members pay by check each month and John recently purchased a new piece of equipment for $15,000. Monthly labor expenses, excluding his manager's salary, are twenty-five percent of sales. John has also refinanced his loan more than once and, after fifteen years, is still making payments of $10,000 each month. John pays himself $180,000 per year. He also has two administrative assistants, each making $35,000. John's 4,000 members on average pay him by the twenty-fifth day of each month, even though the payment is due on the first.

> Jane's facility is two years old and is catching on in her community. Jane currently has 2,400 members who pay $50 each month

for their family memberships. Jane's staff is very new and eager to learn. They are familiar with the preventative maintenance requirements of equipment and have done an excellent job maintaining the quality of the equipment. Jane's manager makes $35,000. Jane's members pay through automatic debit on the fifteenth of each month. Jane also needed to place a large equipment order for $15,000. Labor at Jane's facility, excluding her manager, is twenty-three percent of sales for the month. Jane has diligently paid her loan down and hopes to have her facility paid for in five years. Jane's monthly note is $11,000 per month. Jane pays herself $75,000 per year. Jane has one administrative assistant whom she pays $30,000 per year.

Let's look at each business owner's income statement:

John & Jane Health Club: Income Statement Comparison for one month

	John's Club		Jane's Club	
Total Sales	$120,000		$120,000	
– Cost of Goods	15,000		15,000	
= Gross Profit	105,000		105,000	
Controllable Expenses				
Labor	33,750	32.14%	27,066	25.78%
P/R Taxes	3,037	2.89%	2,756	2.62%
Travel	450	.42%	325	.30%
Advertising	2,700	2.57%	4,200	4.00%
Promotions	1,850	1.76%	700	.66%
Outside Services	1,250	1.19%	1,250	1.19%
Operating Supplies	6,750	6.42%	3,062	2.91%
Maintenance & Repair	5,500	5.23%	3,500	3.33%
Utilities	3,700	3.52%	1,850	1.76%
Office Expense	250	.23%	125	.11%
Cash +/-	20	.02%	100	.09%
Misc. Controllable Exp.	1,000	.95%	1,000	.95%
Total Controllable Expense	60,257	57.39%	45,934	43.75%

Profit after Controllables	44,743	42.61%	59,066	56.25%
Non-Controllable Expenses				
Rent/Loan Payment	10,000	9.52%	11,000	10.47%
Legal/Accounting Fees	500	.47%	500	.47%
Insurance	4,500	4.28%	1,800	.17%
Taxes/Licenses	500	.48%	750	.71%
Depreciation/Amortization	7,500	7.14%	8,500	8.09%
Interest Expense	2,500	2.38%	2,500	2.38%
Misc. Non-Controllable Expense	1,200	1.14%	300	.28%
Total Non-Controllable Expense	26,700	25.43%	25,350	24.14%
Operating Income	18,043	17.18%	33,716	32.11%
General & Administrative Expense				
Officer's Salary	15,000	14.29%	6,250	5.95%
Administrative Wages	5,833	5.55%	2,500	2.38%
Administrative Travel	2,500	2.38%	1,500	1.42%
Meals and Entertainment	1,000	.95%	500	.47%
Pension/Profit Sharing	2,500	2.38%	2,500	2.38%
Other	1,500	1.42%	150	.14%
Total Gen. and Admin. Expense	28,333	26.98%	13,400	12.76%
Net Income	(10,290)	(9.8)%	20,316	19.35%

When evaluating a business, an income statement will tell you part of the story, but the cash flow statement provides even greater detail and may give you better information. For example, on an income statement, if a business makes a sale in a given month, it must be shown as revenue. But check the cash flow statement – if the business has been unable to collect on the sale, it may show a cash flow shortage.

As my last corporate sales job taught me, "A sale isn't a sale until the money is collected." To become a Wealthy Entrepreneur, you not only want to make the sale, but you've got to *get* the money, collected and in the bank.

In our example, John allows his customers to pay by check and many of them take advantage by paying late. All of his payments are received by the twenty-fifth of the month, while Jane's customer payments are received at the same time each month. So which business has better control over its cash flow? Jane's, of course.

What if both businesses were to sell for $700,000. Which business would you buy and why? Some factors you may want to consider include age of the building, the cash flow from operations (Operating Income + Depreciation), sales, memberships, maintenance and repair, management experience, and opportunity for growth.

As you can see from our simple example, there are many factors that influence the viability and long-term profitability of a business. Your ability to drive sales and control expenses will be critical to your success.

Now let's look at the respective cash flows of each business in our example and see how this particular month has affected their positions. Let's assume both businesses had $10,000 cash on hand and $20,000 in the bank to start the month:

Cash Flow Comparison

	John's Cash Flow Chart	Jane's Cash Flow Chart
Cash on Hand	$10,000	$10,000
Cash in Bank	20,000	20,000
Other Cash	0	0
Total Cash Beginning of Month	30,000	30,000
Income During Month	120,000	120,000
Investment Income	100	100
Credit Sales	0	0
Other Income	0	0
Total Income	120,100	120,100
Expenses for Month		
Cost of Goods Sold	15,000	15,000
Total Controllable Expenses	60,267	43,434
Total Non-Controllable Expenses	26,700	25,350
General & Administrative	13,333	7,150
Owners Draw	15,000	6,250
Total Expenses	130,300	97,184
Total Cash at End of Month Balance	19,800	52,916
Change in Position	(10,200)	22,916

As you can see from our example, John's older facility required greater reinvestment and his highly compensated management staff is not managing his expenses. John is also taking a large salary and has substantially more general and administrative expenses than Jane. Consequently, his cash position is dropping.

Jane's newer facility requires less maintenance and repair and, despite having less experience, her managers are more effectively controlling expenses.

Jane's discipline regarding her own pay and her general and administrative lines are helping her business generate positive cash flow.

Having adequate financial reserves is critical. Jane is well on her way to having more than adequate cash reserves and can plan for reinvestments and expansion. John, whose business is aging, will have to borrow to repair his location if his business continues to operate in this fashion.

Many entrepreneurs fall on difficult times because they fail to plan for reinvestments. When the unexpected happens, they have to borrow the money because they've already spent all the money that was in the business.

Remember, our goal is not only to become entrepreneurs, but also to stay in the game for a long, long time. To do that requires discipline, planning, and execution.

There are many people whose businesses are generating adequate cash, but because of their lack of discipline, they are leveraged to the maximum when they should be accumulating wealth. This is no different than being an employee and over-spending or living beyond your means.

STRATEGY 13

CONSIDER FRANCHISING

My approach to franchising was to look at it as one vehicle to use on my road to creating wealth. I looked at it as a fairly safe place to put money to work so I could start building my nest egg. If you're like me and you don't have a lot of experience with starting a business or you don't want the headaches of the traditional start-up, then franchising may be just the vehicle for you as well.

With a franchise, you're not reinventing the wheel, spending time, money, and energy creating a new business model and new systems. When I bought my franchise, what I was really buying were the systems and infrastructure that were already in place, so my business was off and running from the start. That was a great comfort to someone jumping off from a corporate job with a steady paycheck.

As a franchisee, there will be times when you may disagree with the system, may be expected to reinvest, or do whatever the franchiser requests. Although you are an independent businessperson, you are still operating under a corporate umbrella, and at times you may not agree with every move the company makes.

My attitude has always been to put the system first, providing the investment or request won't put me out of business. That doesn't mean I won't speak my mind, voice my opinion, or give alternatives, but most of the time, I go forward with the system in mind.

Most franchisers have some sort of operator leadership council that brings concerns of the franchisees forward. If the company cares about its operator community, it will work in partnership with franchisees to find opportunities together.

In franchising, you're part of a large system of people or independent business owners who conduct business under one brand name. At times, this can be very beneficial. But many customers don't distinguish from one location to the next; they may lump your location in with others owned by different franchisees with whom they've had a negative experience.

Also keep in mind that as part of a franchise system, you do lose some control: hours of operation, supplies, or advertising may not be your call. Independent thinkers who like to do things "their way" may have a tough time in a franchising system.

That's not to say you can't be creative within a franchise system. In fact, you can and you should. No one will know your specific market, customers, or business as well as you do. Magic Johnson, for example, has joint ventures with Starbucks®. What makes his stores unique is that he sells sweet potato pies in a couple of his locations. He understands his market. In his movie theaters in New York, he sells popcorn shrimp because he recognizes that his customers eat *at* the movies rather than before or afterwards. It's this type of understanding and expertise that a franchise owner can bring to the table with people in the corporate office.

I think franchising is a great way for a person who lacks experience to get into the game of business ownership. Yes, you pay for the company's services, but franchising also has a high success rate.

For me, it's been an excellent place to learn business. Now if there are opportunities I'd like to pursue, I at least have the confidence to evaluate their merit. I conduct my due diligence based on previous experience.

Franchising Investments, Fees, and Financials

What are the details you need to be aware of when buying a franchise? There are many! Consider some of the following:

✓ **Cash Investment:** This is when it becomes important to be in control of your finances and your financial documents. You need to understand where this initial investment could come from, and how you can access that cash.

Can your cash investment be borrowed? Some franchises require non-borrowed, unencumbered funds. You may need to decide what you can sell or liquidate to come up with this cash. One piece of advice – don't leverage your home, you need a place to sleep!

✓ **Royalty Fees:** Try to determine whether the franchise's royalty fees are competitive within the industry. Are you getting your money's worth? For the one to four percent you give to the franchiser, make sure you're comfortable with the type of legal, advertising, or other support you're getting in return.

Franchisers make projections for a business based on demographics, traffic patterns, etc.

Find out if they'll renegotiate your royalty fees if their projections are off. You should also learn what support the franchiser will give you if a new location of the same franchise impacts sales in your store.

✓ **Opening Expenses:** When I open a new store, I typically over-staff it for the first four or five months. I want to make sure service doesn't suffer while staff gets properly trained. This may cost me an extra two to three percent in staff expenses. For a major start-up, you'll want a pre-opening event; this can cost several thousand to *hundreds* of thousands of dollars. You also need to think about the grounds around your store, which can run into the tens of thousands of dollars. When I started, I had no idea landscaping was so expensive!

✓ **Equipment Costs and Reinvestments:** Companies are always changing – tinkering with their business model, enhancing their image, and remodeling. As a franchisee, it's smart to keep up with the changes as they come and invest the necessary funds to stay on top of things. That way, when you go to sell, the cost of remodeling the store isn't deducted from your asking price.

~Personal Reflection~

What are the financing terms for your franchise? Can the franchiser assist with the process?

We have a seven-year finance plan for our restaurants. Often, people will decide to finance for ten years. While this financial structure produces better cash flow, it adds on three additional years of debt. The decline in depreciation of assets could also leave you with a tax problem. Because you will have to face these difficult decisions, you should investigate whether the franchiser can assist you with banking relationships, advice, and financing terms.

Who owns the building and land?

In my stores, I own the cash flow but not the buildings or land. This means I have to maximize my cash flow if I want to reinvest in something else. With businesses that own the building and/or land, this *is* their investment. Neither means of creating wealth is better than the other; you just have to determine which is best for you.

When do profit and loss statements need to be provided?

I like to have my P&Ls on a monthly basis so I don't have to guess at how the business is doing. The quicker you can get the financials in hand, the better prepared you will be to take corrective action.

Franchising Operations and Marketing Considerations

It is also wise to give some thought to the operations and marketing details before you invest in a franchise. Again, there are many details to consider; here are some you shouldn't miss:

✓ **Hours of Operation:** As I mentioned, with a franchise, you may not be able to set your own hours of operation. If your store requires long hours, it can take its toll on your home life. You may find that you're required to open early and close late even though you don't have many customers during these hours. If this happens, you will lose some money, but there's not a lot you can do about it.

✓ **Length of Franchise Agreement:** The franchise agreement is the length of time you own the business before the franchise comes in to reassess your property. At the end of this time, you may need to make a substantial reinvestment in your business (i.e. put in new floors, adjust sales territory, improve systems, etc.) in order to sign a new agreement with the franchise. You may not want to do this. Therefore, it is important to understand the length of your franchise agreement because it will ultimately determine your length of time to make money. For example, if you have a twenty-year franchise and your store takes seven years to pay off, then you have thirteen debt-free years in which you can accumulate the most wealth. So, find out what parts of the agreement can be extended and what the terms are for a re-write. And, you should also learn about how the agreement can be revoked – of course, you're not planning on this, but it's something you should know.

✓ **Seasonal Swings:** Most businesses have busy and slow seasons. It's important to understand these up front so you can prepare and protect yourself during slower periods.

✓ **Training:** Make sure the franchiser provides adequate training. Some franchises only require two weeks of training – would that be enough for you to feel comfortable running the business?

The operation may or may not assist with back office training. If not, find a peer with a back office and learn how his or her business operates.

~Personal Reflection~

How are locations franchised?

With a smaller start-up, you may find franchisees are given whole areas where they're required to add several stores in a given time frame. With other companies, you're given a single store. Make sure you understand what's involved.

Also, make sure you understand how protected you are from other franchisees moving into your territory. Different companies have different policies about what area can be protected.

Who supplies the products used in your business?

Understand how the franchiser makes money. If you're required to buy all your products from the company, then its attention may be divided between your success and its own supply goals.

What will generate traffic to my store?

Look for visibility opportunities: shopping centers, schools, bars, etc. You should look for everything around your location that could bring in business.

Also be aware of barriers to store traffic. These might include railroad tracks, an underpass, an overpass, or a long turn lane. If you're buying your store from a previous owner rather than building a new one, then the reputation of the existing store could be a potential barrier. It's very tough to change a bad reputation. That's why you often see "Under New Management" signs when stores change hands – the new owner is trying to distance him/herself from past problems.

How will the business be evaluated by corporate operations?

Make sure you know how frequently you'll be evaluated and whether it will be announced or unannounced. Find out what the process is and find out how you would resolve discrepancies if they arise.

STRATEGY 14

WHAT IS YOUR PLAN? IF YOU DON'T HAVE ONE, GET ONE!

Every business should start with a solid business plan. And don't think of it as a one-time exercise; it should be flexible and should evolve as the business grows.

Recognize that your clients may want something different than what you've planned for. I developed my most recent business plan thinking I'd spend the bulk of my time presenting workshops to prospective small business owners. Today, however, most of my presentations are to financial service executives who want to understand how to sell more effectively to small business owners.

Be flexible, but plan. The greatest benefit you get from planning is the learning that takes place while you're doing it. You may have to revise your plan multiple times with a different focus each time, but think how much you learn while doing it!

What does a successful business plan look like? It should show clear vision; demonstrate to potential lenders or investors that cash flow can support repayment and/or the business has strong potential for return on investment; and highlight the expertise and experience of your management team.

It's extremely important to demonstrate how you determined your projections and to be comfortable with every aspect of your plan – you *will* be thoroughly quizzed about the details by bankers and/or investors.

Each section of the plan should adapt as your business grows and changes. As you begin to use real past performance to calculate your future growth, your plan will become a powerful tool to help you chart your company's future course.

Let's review the sections of the business plan to make sure you're presenting the strongest case for your company's business needs:

a) **Executive Summary:** This is without a doubt the most important section of your business plan. You should place it right after your cover page, even ahead of your table of contents. The executive summary is a quick synopsis of your business plan; it should briefly summarize the key points. Make sure you keep it short – preferably two pages or less. Whether you write it first and use it as a guide to write the rest of the plan, or write it last to make sure you include the most important aspects of the plan, make sure the executive summary is *well* written. You will be judged on how well you present your ideas. Also, use this section to grab your readers' attention. Keep in mind that your audience may be reading several business plans – yours should hold their interest.

Include in your plan:
- ✓ The purpose of your venture.
- ✓ Your management team's experience and why you know you'll be successful.
- ✓ Why your product or service is unique and/or what customer needs you will have to address.
- ✓ Specific goals and strategies.
- ✓ Your financing needs.

~Personal Reflection~

What are your goals for the business?

The executive summary should clearly articulate your goals for the business and how you plan to achieve them.

b) Business Description: This section should summarize your company's history and how you got to the point where you are now. Use relevant past performance data to accurately describe your current position. Be honest about the business; most companies run into problems at some point along the way. Talk about your challenges and how you overcame them.

You may also include a *mission statement* in this section. This is a one-sentence description of your company's business purpose and principles. Some plans also include a *value proposition* – a brief statement about what your product or service does to help the customer.

~Personal Reflection~

What makes you stand out from the competition?

Have you discovered an untapped niche in your industry? Do you solve a problem for customers that your competitors haven't addressed? Describe what's unique about your company.

c) **Marketing Plan:** How will you make your product or service available to customers? This section describes your strategy for marketing your company and its product or service. It includes industry and company analysis, a description of your target market and typical customer, analysis of the competition, and branding and distribution considerations.

~Personal Reflection~

Who is your customer? What's the customer's age, lifestyle, gender, and income level?

The more you know about your customer, the better you can *serve* that customer. I tell my clients to become an expert in their customers' businesses. Read the trade magazines your clients read, attend their conferences, even join their country club if you can. You want to know more about them and their business than they know about themselves. Get inside their skin!

What are your competitor's strengths or weaknesses?

Use your competitor's strong suits and downfalls to your advantage. Is there a customer need that your competitor has failed to address? What positive attributes can you emulate?

I've purchased other speakers' books, products, and materials to gain a better understanding of their marketing and product offerings. I've signed up for their email blasts, called them on the phone, and in some cases, I'd even consider collaborating with them on a project.

Studying your competition can help you better determine what your market wants and how to position yourself. All it takes is a niche to make you rich, so study your competition to figure out how to get paid!

Are there issues such as changing consumer trends or changing government regulations that may impact your business and marketing plan?

Be honest about issues that may negatively impact your future projections. How would you address these issues if they did arise?

d) Financial Plan: This is another very important section of your business plan. The financial information you present here tells your reader what your company has achieved to date and what your future projections are for the business. Make sure you're familiar with all of the information you give, from sales projections to profit and loss statements to future projections. Your reader will want to know how you arrived at these numbers, so you need to show you have a solid understanding of them.

~Personal Reflection~

Have you established a line of credit with your bank or have you discussed this possibility with your bank?

Also, make sure your line of credit is large enough. I had a situation in my own business where I needed to inject a great deal of capital to cover payroll, taxes, supplier bills, and mortgage notes, and I quickly discovered that my current line of credit wasn't large enough. So I had to use my twenty-minute prep time before a speech to fax documents to my bank! Even though I got my finances in order and my speech went well, I certainly learned a lesson in the process!

At the same time, most businesses have slow periods during the year. You need to be prepared for these times *before* they hit so you can protect your business and your family with your credit line.

How fast will your business grow?

Make sure you're using your monthly P&Ls to accurately project future growth.

What are your capital needs and how will the funds be used?

Make sure you spell out for the lender or investor exactly what your financing needs are, and how you'll be spending the money.

e) **Management Background:** This section describes why your management team is qualified to successfully lead this business. List your team's qualifications and any past successes that may be relevant to this company's future goals. Include the key responsibilities of each member of your team.

~Personal Reflection~

What are your accomplishments in this industry? What are your team's accomplishments?

Reflect on how far you've come in your business. Note your achievements and those of your team.

Have you had prior experience projecting sales or cash flow?

Even if you've never owned a business, if you've had relevant prior work experience, you should mention it.

f) Supporting Documents: You might want to include these additional documents as an appendix. This section would include any documents you think would be helpful to your reader's understanding of your business. Documents may include additional financial information, resumes of your management team, and any press coverage you or your company has received.

One common financial document might be a sample pro forma. This is a snapshot of your overall projections, and how you feel your business cash flow will support your request for financing.

Sample Pro Forma:

	Sales (Revenue)	$500,000
Minus	Cost of Goods Sold	-$250,000
Equals	Gross Profit	$250,000
Minus	SG&A	-$200,000
Equals	Net Income	$50,000

~Personal Reflection~

Are your pro formas consistent with industry norms?

Again, make sure you're on top of your numbers. Banks and investors see *a lot* of projections, so they know what the industry norms are. Make sure your numbers are realistic. Your accountant, peers, and research can help you determine the industry numbers.

What is your exit strategy?

It's never too early to think about your strategy for leaving your business, even as you contemplate passing your business along to the next generation. What would happen to the business if you had a catastrophic injury? Would your spouse step in? Do you have an arrangement for succession? These are questions the Wealthy Entrepreneur has thought about and prepared for.

STRATEGY 15

MAKE YOUR BANKER WORK FOR YOU

I'm fortunate to have great relationships with my local banks. I've been able to meet each of the CEOs of my banks and it does make a difference when I'm trying to get something accomplished. I can call them on the phone, and they know who I am.

I recognize this may not be possible with larger institutions, but I do believe in the importance of meeting with local bank officers on a regular basis. I do this to keep them up to date on my business and learn what new product offerings they may have that could be useful to me.

One thing I've learned is that as your business grows, so does your influence with your bank. Leverage that. Your influence can help get you better interest rates, fees, and even better services. This will be helpful to you in the future if you need a new home loan, or if your business is down one quarter and you need some capital to help secure it.

If you are a minority or woman-owned business, ask your bank if it participates in any specialized loan programs. The SBA partners with banks to provide financing in both these categories and you may find a loan with a lower interest rate, or one that requires less initial investment.

~Personal Reflection~

Is your banker on your board of advisors?

Maybe you've never even thought of having a board of advisors. I encourage you to do so, by gathering your attorney, banker, accountant, real estate agent, and/or mentor – people in the best position to advise you on the future course of your business and even your life. This group can often give you advice, provide you with introductions to help improve your business, or present you with opportunities you may not have considered.

How frequently will you meet with your banker?

Establish regular meetings with your banker, one to four times per year. As your business grows, your banking needs may change. You may also find that, in time, you are in a better negotiating position. Find out what other services your bank offers, such as private banking.

How frequently will deposits be made?

I recommend you make deposits frequently. In the event that one of my stores is robbed, my insurance only covers one day's deposits.

Will the bank count your deposits with or without your supervision? How are discrepancies handled?

I'm not that trusting. My bank counts the money in front of my company representative. If there's a discrepancy, we handle it on the spot. Think about how a discrepancy would be handled if you or someone from your company were not there to deal with it.

Who will conduct your banking?

Establish a system. If someone other than you is taking deposits to the bank, how are those deposits being recorded?

Who will have the responsibility of signing checks?

I encourage you to keep check signing authority, especially when you're just starting your business. Be in control. I figure if Oprah Winfrey's been doing it for years, then that's probably a good enough example for the rest of us. (And she was still signing the checks, last I heard.) Even if you trust someone else to do it, you still need to spot check occasionally.

STRATEGY 16

INSURE YOURSELF AND YOUR BUSINESS

If you transition from employee to Wealthy Entrepreneur, I would advise having a complete physical by your physician prior to leaving your current position. Then, check to determine if you can get insurance coverage on your own. After gaining forty pounds, I found it difficult to purchase an insurance policy until my cholesterol and blood pressure levels dropped. This concerned me because I was so highly leveraged with debt, and was working without adequate insurance coverage.

If you have a health condition that may be considered pre-existing, now is the time to determine if this will impact your insurability. Discuss this in detail with your insurance representative. Owning a business is enough risk, opening a business without insurance is insane!

Wealthy Entrepreneurs may carry the following types of insurance: Liability, Property, Umbrella Policy, Employment Practices, Workers Compensation, Medical/Dental, Life, Disability, Auto, Vision, and Health. In addition, they also may have additional personal life insurance and have umbrella policies on their homes.

When searching for an insurance agent, I recommend asking family, friends, or peers for a couple of different names, and make sure the agent is experienced with small business owners.

Insurance companies should have high financial ratings of A+ or higher. While it may be tempting to buy cheaper insurance from a lesser-known company, you may find the prices rising on you and their service sub-par when you really need their help. Then your business will *really* be at risk.

I have added an additional term life insurance policy to cover the debt of our business should anything happen to me, or should my wife decide not to take over the business in case of my death. Many Wealthy Entrepreneurs also carry an additional policy to protect their families from taxes in case of death, when estate tax planning is an issue.

Often overlooked policies are Disability and Business Interruption insurance. Disability insurance is important if, for example, you're an accountant and you become disabled and have no employees. Without this insurance, how will you maintain your lifestyle while you rehabilitate?

Business Interruption insurance will protect

your business when issues outside of your control interrupt your normal operation for an extended period of time. Usually this coverage requires a history of sales/revenues prior to implementation, so check with your agent.

On an annual basis, have your insurance agent review your business and your policies to look for ways to enhance your coverage or lower your premiums. For instance, I have heard of businesses lowering their premiums by creating safety teams that meet regularly and post safety messages to remind workers to avoid slips and falls. Ask your agent if this is something you should consider.

~Personal Reflection~

What is the best type of insurance to purchase?

Consult your financial/professional advisor team to determine which policies you need and what extra ones you should consider. Depending on the business and its location, your needs will be different. But I can't stress enough, you get what you pay for. Find the best! When disasters happen, and unfortunately they will, you want your insurance company to respond ASAP to get you and your business up and running smoothly again. If you can't get in touch with your insurance agent, it doesn't matter how much money you saved. By choosing a sub-par agency, you've now put your business, and consequently your family, in danger.

STRATEGY 17

BECOME INVOLVED IN YOUR COMMUNITY AND GIVE BACK

Giving Back

I belong to the National Black McDonald's®
Operators Association. In September 2005,
Hurricane Katrina leveled the businesses and
homes of five of the association's operators; they
lost everything. By pulling resources together, the
association was able to give these five members a
total of $400,000 to put their lives back together.
We realize we're all small businesses, but collectively
we have a bigger voice, and we can make a
difference.

Community involvement can reap big dividends
for the Wealthy Entrepreneur and you should
not underestimate it. Giving back to your local

community through donations of money, time, or resources is a wonderful and personally fulfilling way to make your community a better place to live.

In addition, by being involved in the community, your business becomes a goodwill ambassador and often will benefit from additional business as a result of your effort to sponsor an event or be involved in a community project.

Embrace the Meet and Greet

Networking often goes hand in hand with community involvement. As I network and meet with different people, my goal is to find possible win-win scenarios. If I meet with someone from an industry or organization I'd like to learn more about, I don't hesitate to call and take him or her out to lunch.

I once took my former PeeWee basketball coach to lunch to learn more about rental real estate in my hometown. He came with his son, who was also in the business, so I asked them both a lot of questions about the risks and rewards of owning rental real estate. As lunch was ending, the coach's son asked for the bill, but I insisted on paying. The son looked somewhat surprised, but the coach knew exactly what I was doing. They had provided me with valuable information, so as a result, I felt obliged to buy lunch, in addition to the rental property I later bought!

Networking is a skill that should be at the top of any Wealthy Entrepreneur's "to do" list. I recently spoke at a business exposition attended by prominent business leaders from around the state. I look at these functions as a great way to build my business, contacts, and relationships. Everyone at this event was focused on business growth. That doesn't happen often, so I really took advantage of the opportunity.

Before I spoke, I called my office and had them bring over two hundred "Be Our Guest" cards to put in each person's seat. By the end of the conference, people remembered me not only as the "Local McDonald's® Owner," but also had a reason to come into my restaurant. This not only helped me make contacts, it also generated business.

Also at the event, I was introduced to two women who worked for the state and who were interested in my seminars. They wanted to see my information, so I hurried back to my office, picked up my media kits, and brought them back to the potential clients. I talked to them about my services and then emailed them later that evening to thank them for their time. When they arrived at work the next morning, my email with a follow-up request to do business was the first thing they saw. By 8:03 a.m., I had a confirmation from them, along with a message that they looked forward to working with me.

You have to be willing to do whatever it takes to be successful. Separate yourself from the pack and be ready to conduct business anywhere, anytime. Networking also gives the Wealthy Entrepreneur the opportunity to get to know people on a personal level, and we all know people do business with people they know and like.

Some quick rules of thumb for networking: be positive, avoid complex or inappropriate topics such as race or sex, don't tell derogatory jokes, and be mindful of your alcohol intake. Remember, your mission is to conduct business. Move your business forward through networking!

Be a Joiner

Joining local organizations is a personal choice; each city has different groups with different criteria. I've been very impressed with my local Chamber of Commerce; it's provided me with numerous personal and professional contacts.

You may find your Chamber of Commerce has awards you can strive for – pursue them! The publicity you may receive can be invaluable for your business. I was fortunate to win the Lexington Chamber's "Minority Business Person of the Year" award. The story was featured on local TV stations and in the newspaper, and the publicity helped get the word out about my business very quickly.

Your Chamber may also have loan programs you can take advantage of. Mine has one for small loans to minority-owned businesses. You can present your business plan directly to the Chamber's decision-making committee, and receive a reply shortly thereafter.

Government Opportunities

Local and state officials can be wonderful resources for small business owners, and many of their services are "free" (paid with taxes). Using resources in your local government can be a huge benefit, not only to you, but also to government leaders. They need to know and understand how their actions will impact you and other small businesses in the community.

Check to see if there are any state or local government agencies that offer tax abatements for your business. If you're relocating the business or creating jobs, you may qualify. Tax savings are also possible if your business is located in an economically depressed area, or so-called Empowerment Zone. I was able to save my business $50,000 in one store by taking advantage of Empowerment Zone tax savings.

~Personal Reflection~

How will you utilize the Small Business Development Center?

Similar to your Chamber of Commerce, the Small Business Development Center can offer great guidance as you set up your new business. The staff can work with you to develop your business plan, challenge your plan's ideas and projections, and offer you one-on-one coaching.

Are you a member of a local charitable or business board?

Again, joining a local charitable or business board of directors can help you build good will in your community, and you never know what might transpire as you work with your chosen organization. Look around for local opportunities to get involved on boards.

Have you contacted the Service Corps of Retired Executives (SCORE)?

This is a great resource for business start-ups. Their mission is to help small emerging businesses become successful.

Are you a member of a professional organization?

If an organization is relevant to your industry, you should be a member. It's a great opportunity to network with people who understand your business and can help you find solutions and new opportunities.

Are your business cards accurate and up to date?

There's nothing worse than having to scratch out the phone number or email address on your card and write in a new one. It's tacky and unprofessional. Also, make sure your cards are clean and undamaged. Remember that your card reflects your business image.

If you are a minority or woman, is your business certified as such?

Obtaining this certification is a long and involved process; you will need ready access to all the important documents we discussed for Strategy 3: three years of tax returns, three years of bank statements, deed to your home, W-2's for the past year, and two to six months of investment account statements.

Certification can be a great leveraging tool that can potentially propel your business to a higher level. Visit the office of the local Minority Supplier Development Council in your city and inquire about the certification process.

STRATEGY 18

UNDERSTAND MINORITY POPULATION TRENDS

In 2003, I had an opportunity to attend a presentation by Magic Johnson where he described his success in taking brands such as Starbucks® and making them relevant to the African American communities he serves. By focusing on the needs of his consumers, his Starbucks® joint ventures are some of the highest grossing stores in that well-known coffee chain.

What Magic does is common sense. When you look at the census data, the real question becomes: Can you afford *not* to pay attention to the minority market and its growing influence?

According to the U.S. Census Bureau's projections:

✓ By 2045, eighty-six percent of the total population growth will come from minority groups (Hispanics, African Americans, Asians, Pacific Islanders, and American Indians).

✓ The combined total of all ethnic minority populations will grow from 79 million in 2000 to 178 million in 2045.

✓ Minority share of the population will increase from twenty-six percent in 2000 to forty-six percent in 2045.

✓ By 2045, minority purchasing power may reach $4.3 trillion.

✓ Minority population may contribute forty-four percent, or as much as seventy percent of the total increase of purchasing power from 2000-2045.

According to U.S. Secretary of Transportation Norman Y. Mineta, "America's population will increase fifty percent over the next fifty years, with almost ninety percent of that increase in the minority community. Both Fortune 1000 and minority businesses need to pay attention to the consumer purchasing power that will result from that growth."

These demographic trends and increases in purchasing power will impact not only purchasing decisions, but also how business is done in this country. It will create enormous opportunities for minority businesses of all sizes.

As a business owner, I have found it necessary to study Spanish language and culture. Although I'm not fluent, I find it helps me communicate better with my Spanish-speaking employees and customers. In turn, I feel it helps my business. I have managers who are Latin and others who are fluent in Spanish; they are great resources to me. The Hispanic community is growing rapidly in size and influence. They are loyal customers. Will your business be positioned to grow as this segment of the population continues to grow?

~Personal Reflection~

What skills or experience do you have marketing to minority groups?

Many industries have difficulty marketing to minority groups because they haven't yet built trust or brand equity with this population. Your involvement in these communities and your consistency will reap dividends for you.

Can you speak a foreign language fluently?

Leverage your skill set. If you speak a foreign language, it may be very useful to you in your business venture.

I recently returned from a trip to China, where it seemed like every high school and college student I encountered was studying English and wanted to practice with me. It was obvious to me that these students really understood the value of learning a second language.

If you have foreign employees, are they fluent in English?

Language barriers can be problematic in a business setting. I find I need to balance the need for diversity in the workplace with the need for English speakers.

If your employees are not fluent in English, is your handbook written in a language they understand?

All my company handbooks are written in English and Spanish. I don't want to have any uncertainty or misunderstandings about my company's employee standards or expectations.

STRATEGY 19

MANAGE YOUR CREDIT AND DEBT OR BECOME AN ECONOMIC SLAVE

My mission is to influence families by spreading the word about business ownership, investing, and long-term planning. Before you can run you must walk, and before you can walk you must crawl. In other words, we need to start slow and build on one success at a time.

In some of my presentations, I give the example that it takes approximately thirty years to pay off a $2,000 credit card bill with an interest rate of nineteen percent if you only make the minimum monthly payment. If there is a cancer to personal wealth, I am convinced that lack of discipline toward installment debt is one of the worst. Companies target you when you're young and vulnerable. If you don't believe me, look at a college campus.

When you're young, you don't have the necessary life experience to foresee the problems your actions can cause. So maybe you graduate from college not only with student loans, but also with installment debt of a few thousand dollars, thanks to all those nights out with friends drinking beer and eating wings. Now you're relocating, often to a new city, in need of a new car, a deposit for an apartment, and furnishings. Suddenly it hits you just how deep in debt you are!

If you find yourself in this or a similar high debt situation and you have multiple credit card accounts, my suggestion would be to first target the highest interest rate account and pay the monthly minimum, plus an extra amount you're comfortable with to reduce and eventually eliminate this debt. Others advise you start with the lowest interest rate card first to establish a successful pattern of eliminating debt. Whichever tactic you choose, start today!

If you have multiple cards, cut up the first one after the debt is eliminated, and return it to the card company with a note indicating you no longer want to use the card.

With your second account, apply the first card's payments (monthly minimum plus the additional amount you applied) against the second card, plus the second card's minimum monthly payment. This will help accelerate your debt payment and save you money in interest.

Then repeat the process on the next card. Eventually, you will eliminate your installment debt and be on your way to financial health. (See the example below.)

Example of how to eliminate credit card debt:

Card	Balance	Minimum Payment	Minimum Payment, Prior Card(s)	Extra Dollar Amount	Total Monthly Payment
No. 1	$ 500	$ 50		$150	$200
No. 2	$1,000	$ 75	$ 50	$150	$275
No. 3	$1,500	$100	$125	$150	$375
No. 4	$2,000	$150	$225	$150	$525

It's a good idea to keep at least one credit card for emergencies, hotel reservations, and airline tickets, but use it responsibly or you will end up on the high debt treadmill. Wealthy Entrepreneurs live below their means and use credit responsibly.

When you pay off your credit card debt and you develop the discipline to pay for expenditures each month, then you should use the excess cash flow to build financial reserves of at least three to six months of income.

~*Personal Reflection*~

Do you have more than three to five credit cards?

You shouldn't! Lenders don't just look at your debt; they also look at the credit you have access to as potential debt. How much credit do you really need? See if you can reduce your number of cards to one or two. Also, check to make sure the cards you *do* have carry competitive interest rates – these can be negotiated. Get into the habit of checking how much you're *actually* spending for the ease of having these cards.

Emergency Cash Reserves/Pay Yourself First

As a Wealthy Entrepreneur, work with your bank or credit union to determine if you can get a money market account with a higher rate of interest and limited check writing. Your goal for this account is to have the money in case of emergency. This cash reserve will take time to build, but be diligent about paying yourself first.

What do I mean by paying yourself first? Before you pay your creditors, you should pay yourself at least ten percent of your take home pay. First, you need to have a S.Y.S.T.E.M (See Yourself Save Ten Percent Each Month). You and your family should be paid first. I hear people say to me all the time, "But I have too many bills." What you're really saying is that your bills are more important than you and your family. Nothing can be *that* important.

I'm not saying don't meet your obligations. If you've gotten yourself into a difficult situation, it's your responsibility to get yourself out. But your family's financial health is also your responsibility, so take care of that first.

Check with your bank or credit union to find out if you can automatically transfer funds from your checking account to your money market or savings account each pay day. Let's say my gross pay is $1,500 every two weeks. On the first and fifteenth I would want $150 automatically transferred into this account. It's easy to establish, so check with your bank. And remember that these funds are for your cash reserve – once they go into this account, they shouldn't be touched. This is not your Christmas fund, vacation money, or down payment for a new car. This is the "beginning of your financial freedom" fund and can't be touched unless there is an emergency, such as a death in the family or a busted water heater.

~Personal Reflection~

Does your income fluctuate?

If you're leaving a corporate job to start your business, you may find that your income from your new venture fluctuates more than you're comfortable with. Try to predict the peaks and valleys of your business and figure out how you're going to manage the tight periods.

Does your spouse/partner work?

When you're starting a new business, it's helpful if your spouse is also working and earning income for the family. If your spouse is working and you can be carried under his or her insurance plan, take advantage of that benefit.

Do you own an older home?

It's wise to put away extra cash for unexpected maintenance and repair costs around the home, whatever they may be.

STRATEGY 20

PLUG YOUR MONEY DRAINS!

I understand that in some personal situations, paying yourself first may be difficult. But I encourage you to use income expense spreadsheets, like the ones shown for Strategy 8 or available through your financial software, to see where your money is going and reduce spending wherever possible. Let's look at some easy ways to find extra cash:

Vending Machines

Let's say you visit the vending machine twice a day and you spend $2 each day. If you work twenty days during the month, it amounts to $40 each month. Pack some snacks or buy them in bulk at the store. You'll save money, and you'll probably have a healthier option than the vending machine offering.

Roll Change

I'm as guilty of this as the next person at times. Let's say each day you have spare change and you throw it into a bucket. It sits there month after month until you finally sit down and roll it and take it to the bank. To your surprise, it totals a couple of hundred bucks. What you need to consider is what was lost: interest and time, both of which mean lost money for you. Roll your spare change regularly, take it to your bank, and put it in your reserve account.

Coupons

Each week my wife grabs the Sunday paper and tears out coupons. It's really not an interest of mine, but she enjoys it. Surprisingly, each month she saves about $50. If you annualize that, it adds up to more than $600!

I also recommend going to the grocery store on a full stomach, bringing a list of items you specifically need, and leaving the kids at home. If I'm hungry and I go shopping, I'm guaranteed to come home with chips, soda, and a bunch of extra food I didn't plan on buying. If I'm hungry and my sons are with me, then back up a tractor-trailer because we'll need it to make a delivery at the Wilkins house! My sons will burn a hole in my wallet because of all the cereal ads they see on television. We end up with four or five different cereals if they go into the store.

Insurance

Work with your insurance company to package your car, home, investment real estate, business, life, and umbrella policies to determine if there are any hidden savings. My wife and I were able to save over $2,000 with our adjusted premiums by packaging our insurance needs.

Telephone

This industry is so competitive today. Look for the best plan for your calling patterns and switch if necessary.

One of my weaknesses is calling information from my cell phone. It's convenient and saves me the trouble of looking up numbers in the phone book. But according to my business manager, my habit of dialing 411 cost me over $600 in unnecessary charges in one calendar year.

I recently purchased a cell phone for my oldest son. The sales manager of a national chain asked me how many phones I use in my business, then mentioned we could save up to twenty-two percent if we combined all of our phones under one umbrella; in addition, we could offer a discounted rate for our employees. Twenty-two percent is a substantial savings, but more importantly, passing on discounts to our employees improves company morale.

Gas & Electric

Turn off lights when you leave a room, check

for drafts and seal them, and use blinds on your windows to keep heat out during the summer and in during the winter. Check with your electric company regarding average billing to determine if that will help your cash flow.

Water

I walk around my house and constantly say to my children, "Save some water for the fish." How often do you let the water run while brushing your teeth or start the shower well before you're ready to get in? Don't waste money by letting the water run. Also, make sure you fix any leaks. If your toilet constantly runs, you're flushing money down the commode. You can save even more on your water bills if you install low-flow faucets and showerheads, with just a little initial investment. You can also fill an old plastic milk jug with some pebbles or sand and water and place it in the tank of your toilet – you'll use substantially less water every flush, which can add up your savings quickly.

Internet

If you have a computer and you use the Internet, send emails instead of calling someone long distance. Consider, "Would I rather pay $20 each month or $100 or more for a phone bill?" My wife uses the Internet daily to communicate with her family in North Carolina, and the savings on our phone bills are noticeable. Some companies are now offering phone services online, sometimes at substantial savings over traditional plans. This might be worth looking into if you or your family really prefer to speak with someone.

Dry Cleaning

There are pros and cons to dry cleaning. Some will say dry cleaning helps your clothes last longer, which might be true. Others will say that by ironing yourself, you save at least a dollar per shirt. One of the best things my mother taught me was how to iron. Use your best judgment, but understand that convenience costs money.

Automobile Purchasing

Growing up, I remember my father driving around in a 1963 Chevrolet. Every time I was in the car, I was so embarrassed I'd crouch down in my seat and hope none of my friends would see me. I asked him why he still drove this old car and his reply was that a car is just transportation to get from point A to point B. He rarely bought new cars, choosing instead to buy good used automobiles. Today, I believe in buying used cars whenever possible and I take pride in driving them for a long, long time. When I left my old employer, I bought my company car, a Ford Explorer. The truck had 85,000 miles when I purchased it. I drove it for another six years, four of them without a payment. When I finally traded it back in to the dealer, it had

190,000 hard-earned miles. Its replacement was a used Explorer demo with 5,000 miles and a reduced price tag.

Buy used cars and let someone else take the hit on depreciation – and in general, don't lease. Your goal is to get out of debt, not to stay in it. There may be situations where leasing makes sense for business purposes, but discuss that option with your accountant before you decide.

Car Maintenance

The only way I was able to rack up 190,000 miles on my old truck was through regular maintenance. I am a big believer in routine oil changes every 3,000 miles. Oil to a car is like cash to a business. They both need it to run.

I would rather spend $50 every four months than thousands for a new engine or some problem that could have easily been prevented. Take care of your car, pay it off, and go to the bank!

Each time I had my oil changed, I sighed in relief that it was only $50 instead of $500. That's a big difference and you can increase your net worth quickly with that type of savings each month.

Review Your W-4

If you get big tax refunds each year, you may want to review your withholding. When you receive a refund, it really means you were giving the government an interest-free loan. That's money you and your family could have been using earlier to create your cash reserves, fund your retirement, or to create generations of wealth. I'd rather have $1,000 earning eight percent in my mutual fund account than have it sitting in the government's account gaining no interest.

Take Your Legal Deductions

If you give to charities, own a home, and/or have children, these factors may provide you with legal deductions. As a Wealthy Entrepreneur, save your records and have tax strategies year-round. If you donate to a church or a non-profit cause, get a statement of your contributions so that you have a record of your deductions.

Private Mortgage Insurance

If you own a home and you put down less than twenty percent to purchase the property, there's a good chance you owe Private Mortgage Insurance (PMI). PMI is used to guarantee the banks their investment return should you default. PMI helped you purchase your dream home, but it might be time to have your home appraised to determine if your equity is at or above twenty percent. Your equity in real estate increases as a result of paying down your mortgage or property appreciation. Once your equity is above twenty percent, you can usually cancel the PMI – do this as soon as possible to avoid paying the monthly fee when you don't need to. This savings each month could be used to build your emergency or investment funds.

~Personal Reflection~

What do you need *versus* what do you just want?

When you make a purchase, are you really buying an asset or a liability? When I go to make a purchase, I often ask myself, "Do I want this or do I *need* this?" It takes some inner strength, but I've often walked away, knowing the item in question was just something I really *wanted*.

Do you think in the long-term?

If I have extra cash, I immediately think, "Asset or liability?" What am I going to do with this money? If my goal is to create wealth and provide options for my children, then the excess cash is easily deposited into a mutual fund or some investment that will generate additional wealth.

Unfortunately, many people are not long-term thinkers and instead go for instant gratification, convincing themselves they're buying an asset. When I say asset, I mean something that will appreciate in value and may offer some sort of dividend, rent, or royalty payment.

So let's say you've learned all the tricks on how to save cash and you've eliminated your debt outside of your home. Now you can begin to create a diverse wealth system.

STRATEGY 21

CREATE A DIVERSE WEALTH SYSTEM

When a system is in place, it is regular, routine, and occurs without thought. In my opinion, the average person doesn't have time, knowledge, or understanding to select stocks and to time the market for investments. Therefore, most people need to establish a system of investing that is consistent with their goals of creating generations of wealth.

A diverse wealth system is a systemic way of investing that creates wealth from stocks, bonds, businesses, real estate, and other appreciable assets. The objective is to create streams of wealth from a variety of vehicles. Let's look at the options:

Investments
Stocks

When you own a share of a company's stock, you

own a piece of that company. There are numerous ways to make money with stocks, but I'm going to stick to the basics. (For greater depth, talk to your financial advisor.) Theoretically, stocks should increase in value as the company's earnings grow. In addition, many stocks pay dividends each quarter. If your company or broker holds your stock in a dividend reinvestment plan, the dividend can be automatically reinvested in additional shares to create greater wealth.

Let's say you bought 100 shares of Microsoft at $25 per share. In three months the stock is now at $30, so your investment is now worth $3,000. In addition, Microsoft declares a quarterly dividend of 0.25 per share, so you take 0.25 X 100 shares and we receive an additional $25. So for the quarter, your investment increased in value by $525, or twenty-one percent, minus any fees charged by the brokerage company.

It would take about twenty years to make that much in a bank at today's interest rates!

Bonds

When you own a bond, you are loaning money to an entity, municipality, or government. In return, the organization will pay you interest on that money and also set a date in the future when they will reimburse you your principal. That is called the maturity date. Bonds can be sold before their maturity dates to other investors and this may generate a capital gain if the selling price is higher than the purchase price or a capital loss if it is less, so talk to your financial advisor to determine your strategy.

Most bonds pay interest two times per year, so let's say you bought a $5,000 bond at five percent interest. You would receive interest payments of $125 in June and December.

Bonds are sold individually and also in mutual funds, so if you're interested in bonds consider all purchasing alternatives.

Mutual Funds

I am like most individuals; I don't have the time, knowledge, or skill to keep up with the stock market every day of the week. For that reason, I primarily invest in mutual funds. Mutual funds pool investors' money together, invest in multiple companies to reduce risk, and are run by investment professionals. However, each fund has its own objective and it is up to you to conduct your due diligence to determine if a particular fund meets your investment objective.

Many people invest in a no-load, low-expense fund, meaning the fund doesn't charge a fee for investing and the fund's total expenses are below one percent of the total fund value. Others are comfortable paying an up-front sales charge. I would suggest reviewing the turnover ratio, which describes how actively the managers trade stocks. Understanding how frequently an account is traded is important. If your stocks are in a taxable income account versus a self-directed IRA, you may be exposing yourself to tax liabilities. So read the prospectus carefully before you invest, and check with your financial advisor!

When looking at the history of a fund, I look long-term. I want a fund that provides a solid return over a ten-year period. Many funds, as a result of their objectives, might hit a home run over a three or five-year period but lose a considerable amount of value over a longer period of years. So look at the longest spectrum possible.

Retirement Plans

Many companies offer retirement vehicles for their employees. These plans are an excellent way to build wealth. With each payroll deduction, you can put money into money market accounts, mutual funds, or whatever your company offers or you designate to offer your employees.

The dollar amount you can put into your retirement vehicles and the rate of matching contributions may vary, so check with your financial advisor to learn the maximum you're allowed by law. But even if you can't contribute the full amount, you should at least contribute whatever amount your plan will match.

One thing you need to consider is the pre-tax benefit of your retirement saving program. Saving pre-tax dollars allows you to save more without feeling the financial impact after taxes. So if you're going to stretch, stretch here to prepare for your retirement. As we know, Social Security is no longer guaranteed, nor are pensions from corporations, so having a self-directed retirement plan is a good benefit for your long-term wealth.

As a contributor to an IRA or 401k, the one drawback is the penalty for early withdrawal. Contributions to these plans may not be withdrawn before the age of 59½. If you do tap the account before then, you need to return the borrowed money within sixty days or face a ten percent penalty as well as a tax penalty.

My company offers a 401k, which is a great thing for my wife and me. We contribute the maximum allowed by law and the company matches dollar-for-dollar on the first four percent of contributions. So now we are not only gaining equity in our business each month, but we're also receiving tax benefits from owning our own business, and we contribute to an outside fund for our retirement. There are many ways to become wealthy by owning your own business.

Excess Cash

Now that you have excess cash reserves and are paying yourself first through your retirement plan, you can begin to invest each month.

When it comes to investing, I try to keep it simple. I don't have time or the understanding to scour over the hottest stocks. I utilize my financial experts. I buy solid companies and mutual funds that I know and respect. And, I use dollar cost averaging, meaning I buy the stock on a regular basis, no matter if the stock market is up or down, and I rarely sell.

I stay in the market and I stay my course through

good times and bad. I am not a get-rich-quick type of person. I believe disciplined and consistent investing in stocks, bonds, mutual funds, businesses, and real estate will help me reach my goals and create generations of wealth.

Real Estate

Rental real estate is exciting to me because I get to use other people's money to pay for my investment. With rental property, your tenants pay monthly rent, which hopefully covers your expenses, plus leaves excess reserves for reinvestment. You are putting a relatively small amount of your personal money at risk to buy a large asset. For example, if you wanted to buy $100,000 worth of stock, you would have to put in that amount of money. In real estate, you might put in $20,000 or less.

So if I had $100,000 to invest, I might be able to control close to $1 million worth of property and use my tenants' and banker's money to leverage the deal.

In addition to leverage, you gain depreciation, appreciation, tax advantages, cash flow, wealth, and ... well, yes, sometimes a call in the middle of the night. I try to limit that by having a property management company who handles the property. I give up some profit, but I maintain my freedom.

I have a good friend who began buying real estate twenty years ago. He purchased one house and rented it to students. After two or three years he was ready to purchase another, so he forked out some cash and did the same.

The next year he wanted another property,

so he borrowed some of the equity from the first house, raised its rent, and took the proceeds from the equity loan to buy his third property. He did all this and put a small amount of money in his pocket – tax-free.

Today, he has more than sixty properties and his rents exceed $1 million annually. Does he spend all of that money? No, he reinvests a large portion each year to keep the properties looking attractive to his rental market. Today, his daughter is the manager for all his properties.

My entry into rental real estate was a duplex in a college setting. As I mentioned, I hired a professional management team to handle complaints, collect rent, and answer all the calls I knew I couldn't handle. However, if you are handy, have a contract that has been reviewed by an attorney, and don't mind the disruptions of showing a property, then save the money and do it yourself.

As a Wealthy Entrepreneur, plan for a rate of vacancy and have a reinvestment plan. Even if the property stays rented for the first ten years and the renter takes care of all repairs, by reserving some of your cash flow you are running your business responsibly.

As always, check with your financial advisors to determine the legalities and strategies of investing in real estate.

Network Marketing

Although I am not in a network marketing program, I think there are classic advantages to participating, such as the low cost of entry and the ability to pass on the business to heirs. We have all been approached by the supercharged network marketing rep who is making hundreds of thousands of dollars annually. But, even if you make only $500 a month and invest it annually in a mutual fund or eventually buy real estate, that little sum of money will help the average person build wealth. It often doesn't take a lot to get a network marketing program going, just your ability to network (often after work hours) and overcome rejection (because you *will* encounter rejection occasionally). If you continue with a program for ten years and use leverage or other people's money, you will build a substantial net worth.

Many Wealthy Entrepreneurs of network marketing businesses create limited liability companies and operate them just as a small business owner would. Check with an attorney before you invest and make sure you understand the system (how it works and how you are paid), the products or services that are being sold, and whom you represent.

Wills and Estate Planning

Many people fail to protect their loved ones from unnecessary stress by not having a will or trust in place at the time of their death. I encourage every Wealthy Entrepreneur to have at the minimum a will and, if your net worth is substantial, a trust.

The key to these documents is that your wishes will be carried out at the time of your death. It could also save your family a lot of unnecessary money, time, and sadness later. If you don't plan correctly, your family may be forced to sell the business you worked so hard to build. So do the right thing now and protect your loved ones.

The Magic of Compound Interest and Time

Earlier in the book, I mentioned that while I was at Procter & Gamble, I was taught the magic of compound interest through the Rule of 72 – that you divide 72 by your rate of interest and your money should double in that many years.

For example, if you had a mutual fund appreciating eight percent annually, then your investment should double in value every nine years. What we didn't factor into the equation was inflation and the impact it has on your savings.

Let's assume you are 25 years old and you're beginning to save ten percent, or $3,000, of your annual $30,000 salary in your company's 401k program. What is the impact of tax-deferred growth, compound interest, and time?

By age 30, you would have $23,146. By age 40, you'll have accumulated $107,849, and by age 65, that money would reach the value of $1,327,777. You would have invested $120,000 of your own money and, through compounding, would earn $1,207,777. You would not owe taxes on those gains until you began to withdraw the money at age 65.

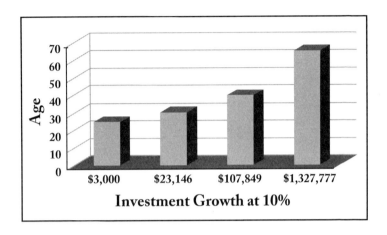

Investment Growth at 10%

Let's assume you decide to invest in more conservative investments and you earn an eight percent return instead of ten percent. What is the financial impact?

Investing your $3,000 at an eight percent return, by age 30 you would have $22,007. By age 40 you would have accumulated $90,972, and by age 65 your investment would total $777,169, for a difference of $550,608.

A two percent change in return over a long period of time can make a significant difference. Many people don't invest aggressively enough and subsequently their portfolios and, more importantly, their lifestyle and families suffer.

The Impact of Taxes on Your Investment Strategy

In our previous example, both of these investments were in tax-deferred accounts. The contributions and gains were free of taxes. The other nice thing about tax-deferred plans like our above 401k example is that they reduce your taxable income, which ultimately puts more money in your pocket in the present.

Let's look at the impact taxes have on your earnings if you were to take those same two investments and put them in taxable accounts instead of investing in a tax-deferred account.

Everything stays the same with the exception of tax-deferred growth. You're 25, contributing $3,000 annually to a mutual fund earning a ten percent return. What impact will taxes have on your investment?

By the age of 30, your investment will be valued at $21,568 vs. $23,146 in the tax-deferred account. By the age of 40, though, the gap begins to widen. Your investment at 40 in the taxable account will be worth $85,070 versus $107,849 for a difference of $22,778, and by 65 the value in your taxable account would equal $630,659 instead of $1,327,777. This represents a loss of $697,118 in wealth.

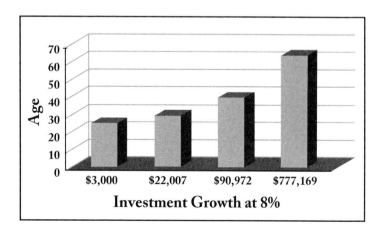

If you can legally save yourself $697,000 in wealth, shouldn't you do so? Talk to your financial advisor to determine if you are maximizing your tax-deferred contribution options.

The other issue this brings to light is the impact time has on your investments. The longer your money stays invested, the more compound interest has time to work. That is why financial advisors tell you that the time to invest is now!

One area that can't be forgotten is inflation. If inflation rises at three percent annually, then your investment options should have a greater return than inflation, otherwise you are losing ground.

Please consult with your investment advisor; the examples I've provided are for illustrative purposes only.

Create Your Own Strategy for Success

An individual with an investment strategy has created *diverse* sources of *wealth*. Some of his or her income may come from a primary job or business, dividends from mutual funds and investments, royalties from licenses or patents, and rental income from real estate.

My point is that you can often find money by simply reviewing your spending and making disciplined small investment decisions that will significantly impact your wealth.

~Personal Reflection~

So what's my strategy?

My strategy might not be right for you and is only intended to be used as an example. One thing I've learned from my business is to think systematically. With a system, things become routine, and if they're routine, they become easy. If systems are easy to follow, then the probability for success is high.

As Wealthy Entrepreneurs, my wife and I both draw salaries from the company and we both participate in our own 401k up to the maximum the law allows. We pay ourselves what we *need* and we look for opportunities to add assets to our portfolio.

Each month, we invest regularly. It's automatic and we don't miss it. We have created a system.

In addition, we have eliminated our credit card debt and have no outside debt other than our businesses. We created a limited liability company and have purchased some real estate properties under it. My goal is that the LLC eventually will have a greater net worth than our primary business.

I also have an obvious passion for my consulting practice and, as it grows, we would like to take the proceeds from this venture and invest in stocks, bonds, and additional real estate. Since we do not have a pension plan, we are attempting to create our own through rental real estate and dividend income.

As always, consult your legal and financial advisors before you make any investment. I hope you have enjoyed this book, and I also invite you to visit our website at www.philwilkins.com.

Resources

Visit our website at www.philwilkins.com

Area Small Business Development Centers
    Provides assistance for entrepreneurs with free/low-cost seminars. Provides assistance with feasibility studies, business planning, and preparation.

Chamber of Commerce
    Excellent source of information/seminars and networking opportunities.

Minority Supplier Development Council
    Assists minority businesses with certification. Assists minority businesses with programs to become more successful. Assists large corporations with strategies on how to use more minority supplier businesses.

Office of Economic Development, State & Local Governments

Manages enterprise zone, has small business loan program, and recruits businesses to the area.

Recommended Reading — Books

Allen, Robert G. *Multiple Streams of Income: How to Generate a Lifetime of Unlimited Wealth.* **Wiley, 2004.**
> An easy-to-read book that describes how to create multiple streams of income and wealth.

Applegate, Jane. *201 Great Ideas for Your Small Business.* **Bloomberg Press, 1998.**
> A surprisingly good book that will give you workable ideas to utilize in your business.

Fraser, Jill Andresky. *The Business Owner's Guide to Personal Finance.* **Bloomberg Press. 2002.**
> An outstanding resource for anyone who is self-employed.

Friedman, Jack P. *Dictionary of Business Terms (Barron's Business Dictionaries).* **Barron's Educational Series, 3rd edition, 2000.**
> A comprehensive dictionary of common business terms.

Gerber, Michael E. *The E Myth.* **HarperCollins Publishers, 1988.**
> A book that will help you plan a systemic approach to operations.

Graham, Stedman. *You Can Make It Happen: A Nine Step Plan for Success.* **Free Press, 1998.**
> A surprisingly good motivational book.

Hanson, Mark Victor, and Robert G. Allen. *The One Minute Millionaire: The Enlightened Way to Wealth*. Harmony, 2002.
   A fun book to read about becoming a millionaire.

Harris, Wendy. *Against All Odds: Ten Entrepreneurs Who Followed their Hearts and Found Success*. John Wiley & Sons, 2001.
   Stories of ten entrepreneurs who overcame great odds to achieve success.

Kiyosaki, Robert. *Cash Flow Quadrant: Rich Dad's Guide to Financial Freedom*. Warner Business Books, 2000.
   Describes four quadrants of business and their advantages and disadvantages: Employee, Self-Employed, Business Owner, and Investor.

Kiyosaki, Robert. *Rich Dad Poor Dad: What the Rich Teach Their Kids About Money – That the Poor and Middle Class Do Not!* Warner Business Books, 2000.
   A great motivational business book describing the benefits of business ownership.

Kroc, Ray. *Grinding It Out: The Making of McDonald's*. St. Martin's Paperbacks, 1992.
   A fascinating book detailing the trials and tribulations of the founder of McDonald's®.

Lesonsky, Rieva, and the staff of *Entrepreneur Magazine. Start Your Own Business*. Entrepreneur Press, 2004.

The Oasis Press. *Smart Start Your Kentucky Business*. Oasis, 2nd edition, 1997.
> An excellent guidebook that provides a comprehensive plan for starting your small business.

Penwell, Tracy L. *The Credit Process: A Guide for Small Business Owners*. Federal Reserve of New York, 1994.
> Provides great information from a bank's perspective.

Savage, Terry. *The Savage Truth on Money*. Wiley, 2001.
> A good book on personal financial planning. Covers all areas of financial planning such as Education, Retirement, and Wills & Estate Planning.

Shemin, Robert, Esq. *Secrets of a Millionaire Real Estate Investor*. Kaplan Business, 2000.
> An easy-to-read guide for real estate investors to follow.

Stanley, Thomas J. and William D. Danko. *The Millionaire Next Door*. Pocket, 1998.
> Describes the surprising spending and thinking habits of millionaires.

Thomsett, Michael C. and Jean Freestone Thomsett. *Getting Started in Real Estate Investing.* **Wiley, 1998.**
Another great real estate book.

Thompson, George B. *Millionaires in Training: The Wealth Builder.* **Prosperity Publishing, 2000.**
A great resource for the beginning investor.

Recommended Reading — Magazines

Black Enterprise Magazine
Provides general information to the African American entrepreneur on a variety of topics such as financial planning, business, and investing.

Fortune Small Business (FSB)
A great magazine with a wealth of articles for a small business owner.

Money
A financial magazine that highlights small business owners and provides valuable financial insights for individuals and families.

Smart Money
A magazine that frequently publishes articles on small business or usable financial information.

Entrepreneur
A great magazine for entrepreneurs.

Opportunities World Magazine

Websites

www.philwilkins.com

Provides links to other sites and regular updates on a variety of topics.

www.sba.gov

A wealth of information on this site.

www.entrepreneur.com

An online version of the magazine. Great articles and help in all areas of business.

www.business.gov

U.S. Business Advisor. A one-stop-shop for information regarding federal government information, services, and transactions.

www.score.org

Retired and active executives provide free, confidential, face-to-face and email business counseling to America's entrepreneurs.

www.quicken.com

Provides articles and assistance on startup and growth of your business, as well as financial matters such as tax planning.

www.IRS.com

Provides a free CD with great information regarding entity selection. You can order up to five each. Give them as Christmas gifts.

www.bls.gov

U.S. Bureau of Labor Statistics. A great resource for employment data.

www.experian.com

A place to visit to receive a copy of your credit report.

www.transunion.com

A place to visit to receive a copy of your credit report.

www.equifax.com

A place to visit to receive a copy of your credit report.

Glossary of Popular Business Terms

Accounts Payable: Debts currently owed by a person or business.

Accounts Receivable: An amount due from customers for products or services purchased.

Accrue: To include an event on the accounting records regardless of whether any cash changed hands. For example, invoices recently sent out would count as income even though customers have not yet paid. Also known as "accrual method." Often used by businesses.

Adjusted Basis: When the original cost of a real estate or other asset is reduced by depreciation or increased expenditures; used to measure gains and losses for tax purposes.

Affirmative Action: Steps taken to correct conditions resulting from past discrimination or from violations of law, particularly with respect to employment.

Amortize or Amortization: Periodic charges or payments to reduce debt, such as debt service on business loans.

Annual Debt Service: Required annual principal and interest payments for a loan.

Bad Debt: A debt that is not collectible and is therefore worthless to the creditor.

Balance Sheet: A financial statement listing a company's assets, liabilities, and equity on a specific date. The left (debit) side of a balance sheet states assets; the right (credit) side shows liabilities and owner's equity. The two sides must equal (balance).

Bankruptcy: An inability to pay debts. Two kinds of Bankruptcy include Chapter 7 (involuntary) and Chapter 11 (voluntary).

Barter: Trade of goods or services without use of money.

Basis: Amount usually representing the taxpayer's cost in acquiring an asset.

Break Even: The point at which revenues equal costs. All sales over the break-even point produce profits; any drop in sales below that point will produce losses.

Cash Basis or Cash Method: Accounting method used by most individual taxpayers. The cash method recognizes income and deductions when money is actually received or paid.

Cash Flow: Incoming cash minus the outgoing cash during a given period.

Cash-on-Cash Return: Divide the annual dollar income by the total dollar invested; a $10,000 investment that pays $1,000 annually would have a 10 percent cash-on-cash return.

Cash Ratio: The assets your business can immediately convert to cash, such as checking accounts, securities, and money market accounts.

Cash Reserve: Cash kept by a person or business that is beyond his or her immediate needs.

Controllable Expenses: Expenses that can be controlled by the department involved; unlike a fixed cost such as rent, which is contracted by lease in advance.

Cost of Goods Sold: A figure representing the cost of buying raw materials and producing finished goods. Included are clear-cut factors such as direct factory labor, as well as others that are less clear, such as overhead.

Credit: Loans, bonds, charge account obligations, and open account balances with commercial firms.

Creditor: One to whom money is owed by the debtor; one to whom an obligation exists.

Debit: Accounting entries on the left side of the general ledger. Debits include the acquisition cost of assets and amounts of deductible expenses.

Debt: Obligation to pay.

Debt Service: Cash required in a given period, normally one year, for payments of interest and current maturities of principal on outstanding debt. Debt Service in mortgage loans includes interest and principal.

Debt to Equity Ratio: Total liabilities divided by total shareholders' equity. This shows to what extent owners' equity can cushion creditors' claims in the event of liquidation.

Deductible: In a tax return, applies to an expense that may be subtracted from income.

Depreciate: Systematically write off the cost of an asset over a period of time allowed by tax law. For example, owners of most commercial buildings can depreciate the building's cost over 39½ years.

Due Diligence: Making a reasonable effort to provide accurate, complete information. An analysis that often precedes the purchase of property or the underwriting of a loan or investment. This analysis considers the financial, physical, legal, and social characteristics of the property and expected investment performance.

Earned Income: A tax term describing "sweat of the brow" income, which requires obvious work on the part of the recipient.

Embezzlement: Fraudulent appropriation, for one's own use, of property lawfully in one's possession; a type of larceny.

Enterprise Zone: A designated area within which businesses enjoy favorable tax credits and other advantages, such as planning exceptions. Enterprise Zones are generally found in inner urban districts that have experienced significant employment declines.

Entrepreneur: An individual who initiates business activity. The term is often associated with one who takes business risks.

Equity: Residual ownership, property value in excess of debt.

First in First Out (FIFO): Method of inventory valuation in which cost of goods sold is determined by assuming that the first unit that ends up in inventory is purchased "first," and in which inventory contains the most recently purchased or produced materials.

Fixed Cost: Cost that remains constant regardless of sales volume. Fixed costs include salaries of executives, interest expense, rent, depreciation, and insurance expenses.

Fixed Expenses: Expenses that remain the same regardless of production or sales.

Gross Profit: Difference between revenue (sales) and the cost of goods sold.

Highly Leveraged: A business or investment financed to a large degree using borrowed funds. High leveraging increases financial risk and the potential for gains and losses.

Income Statement: Financial statement that gives a company's sales, expense, and net income or loss for a specific time period. Income Statements are also referred to as earnings reports, operating statements, or profit and loss statements.

Leverage: Use of borrowed funds to increase purchasing power and, ideally, to increase profitability and wealth.

Liability: Money owed to creditors.

Limited Liability: No personal liability and financial liability can exceed amount invested. Limited liability is provided to stockholders of a corporation and limited partners of a limited partnership.

Limited Liability Company (LLC): Organization form in some states that may be treated as a partnership for federal tax purposes and has limited liability protection for the owners at the state level. The entity may be subject to the state franchise tax as a corporation.

Limited Partnership: Entity in which one or more persons with unlimited liability, called general partners, manage the partnership, while one or more other persons contribute only capital. Limited partners have no right to participate in the management and operation of the business and assume no liability beyond the capital contributed. A limited partnership is often used for real estate ownership because of favorable tax treatment allowing pass-through of losses and avoiding double taxation of income.

Long Term Liability: Liability due in a year or more.

Mission Statement: Definition of a corporation's vision and values. The mission statement typically emerges as part of the strategic planning process.

Negative Cash Flow: Situation in which a business spends more cash than it receives through earnings or other transactions in an accounting period.

Negative Working Capital: Where current liabilities of a firm exceed its current assets. Unless corrected, it may result in bankruptcy.

Net Assets: Difference between a company's total assets and liabilities, owner's equity, or net worth.

Net Income: Sum remaining after all expenses have been met or deducted; synonymous with new earnings and with net profit or net loss depending on whether the figure is positive or negative.

Net Loss: When expenses for the period exceed income for the same period.

Net Operating Income: Income from property or businesses after operating expenses have been deducted, but before deducting income taxes and financing expenses (interest and principal payments).

Net Profit: Amount of money earned after all expenses.

Networking: Making use of professional contacts.

Net Working Capital: Current assets minus current liabilities.

Product Liability Insurance: Coverage usually provided under the comprehensive general liability insurance that also can be purchased separately.

Profit and Loss Statement (P&L): Summary of the revenues, costs, and expenses of a company during an accounting period; also called income statement, operating statement, statements of profit and loss, or income and expense statement.

Pro Forma: Presentation of data, such as a balance sheet or income statement, where certain amounts are hypothetical.

Quick Ratio: Cash, marketable securities, and accounts receivable divided by current liabilities. Excludes inventories.

S Corporation: Corporation with a limited number of stockholders (seventy-five or fewer) that elects not to be taxed as a regular corporation and meets certain other requirements. Shareholders include in their personal tax returns their pro rata share of capital gains, ordinary income, tax preference items, and so on. This form avoids corporate double taxation while providing limited liability protection to shareholders of a corporation.

Section 1031: A section of the internal revenue code that deals with tax-free exchanges of certain property. General rules for a tax-free exchange of real estate are that the properties must be (1) exchanged, (2) like kind property, and (3) held for use in a trade or business or held as an investment.

Selling, General, and Administrative Expenses: A grouping of expenses reported on a company's profit and loss statement between cost of goods sold and income deductions. Included are salespersons' salaries and commissions, advertising and promotion, travel and entertainment, office payroll, and executives' salaries. SG&A expenses do not include financing costs or income taxes.

Service Corps of Retired Executives (SCORE): A volunteer organization of active and retired businesspersons who provide free management advice to small business people.

Sole Proprietorship: A business entity where the owner is taxed at the personal income tax rate and assumes all liability.

Start-Up Costs: Expenditures incurred prior to opening a business.

Sweat Equity: Value added to a property by improvements resulting from work performed personally by the owner.

Triple Net Lease: A lease by which the tenant pays all operating expenses of the property. The landlord receives a net rent.

Variable Cost/Expenses: Business costs that increase with production or sales.

About the Author

Phil Wilkins is a speaker, consultant, and author. He owns three businesses: a training and consulting organization; a group of four McDonald's® restaurants in Lexington, Kentucky; and a real estate investment company.

Phil graduated from Miami University of Ohio in 1986, and began working for Procter & Gamble as a manager in the Finance and Accounting division. In 1988, Phil left Procter & Gamble and began working for Baxter Healthcare, where he was an award-winning sales professional, trainer, and manager. In 1996, Phil left Baxter and began his McDonald's® career in July of 1997.

Phil brings a unique perspective to his speaking, having been a corporate executive and a business owner who operates within a corporate system. The application of his message is practical, easy to understand, and, most importantly, easy to implement.

Commerce Lexington recognized Phil's restaurant business as the Minority Business of the Year in 2004. Phil was also named The Small Business Person of the Year (Runner Up) 2004 for the Commonwealth of Kentucky by the Small Business Administration.

Currently, Phil sits on the Board of Directors for the National Black McDonald's® Operators Association, Commerce Lexington, North Lexington YMCA, and Kentuckiana Minority Business Council of Fifth Third Bank of Central Kentucky, and the Kentucky Minority Business Council. He is a member of the National Speakers Association.

He and his wife Sandi have three children and in his free time, he enjoys playing with his sons, reading, exercising, and practicing Krav Maga, a military fighting technique.

Phil speaks to Fortune 500 companies and non-profit organizations on topics such as High Achievement/Balanced Lifestyles, Teamwork, Leadership, and Business Growth & Development. He is available as a keynote speaker for conventions, seminars, and organizations. If you would like to discuss a possible speaking engagement or obtain additional copies of this book, contact Phil at:

Diverse Wealth Systems, LLC
1035 Strader Drive, Suite 150
Lexington, KY 40505
859-422-2251 or 888-663-6254 phone
859-252-1198 fax
www.philwilkins.com